Learning to Walk

For thirty years Sangharakshita has been playing an important part in the spread of Buddhism throughout the modern world. He is head of the Western Buddhist Order (Trailokya Bauddha Mahasangha), and is actively engaged in what is now an international Buddhist movement with centres in thirteen countries worldwide. When not visiting centres he is based at a community in Norfolk. His writings are available in eleven languages.

Learning to Walk

Sangharakshita

Windhorse Publications

Published by Windhorse Publications
136 Renfield Street
Glasgow G2 3AU

© Windhorse Publications 1990

Cover design Dhammarati

Printed by Dotesios Ltd, Trowbridge, Wiltshire

British Library Cataloguing in Publication data
Sangharakshita, *Bhikshu, Sthavira*, 1925—
Learning to Walk 1. Buddhism:
Sangharakshita, *Bhikshu, Sthavira*, 1925—
I. Title
294.3092
ISBN 0-904766-45-4

Contents

Introduction

'Why don't you write *your* autobiography?'

The speaker was the burly, forty-year-old English doctor who, for the last five or six months, had been staying with me at the Triyana Vardhana Vihara, the monastery I had founded on the outskirts of Kalimpong, a small town in the foothills of the eastern Himalayas, some two years earlier. During those months he had, at my suggestion, written his autobiography, to which he had given the title *Out of the Ordinary* (he was a transsexual and a former disciple of the notorious Lobsang Rampa), and now he was suggesting that I should write *my* autobiography.

'But what would be the point?' I protested. 'I haven't had nearly such an interesting life as you. In fact, my life has been quite ordinary, and even if I did manage to write my autobiography who on earth would want to read it?'

'Nonsense!' retorted my friend, in his usual brusque fashion. 'You've had a *very* interesting life, and if you were to write your autobiography a lot of people would want to read it. It might even become a best-seller.'

I remained unconvinced. I had suggested that Jivaka (at his request I had given him a Buddhist name shortly after his arrival) should write his autobiography because there were, I suspected, things he needed to get off his chest, and writing his autobiography seemed a good way for him to do this. In my own case no such consideration applied.

There was nothing of a personal nature of which I particularly wanted to disburden myself. However, Jivaka returned to the attack, pointing out that I was not very busy just then, and the following morning I therefore sat down at my desk and cast my mind back to my childhood in faraway Tooting.

This was in 1959, and in the course of the next two years I produced about 100,000 words. Not that the work of producing them proceeded uninterruptedly. During the same period I undertook a number of extensive lecture tours in the plains, some of which kept me away from Kalimpong for months together. Then in 1962 I was invited to contribute the articles on Buddhism to the *Oriya Encyclopaedia* and put aside other literary work in order to concentrate on this project. In the course of writing, these articles far outgrew their original purpose, and the first of them was eventually published as *The Three Jewels* and the second as *The Eternal Legacy*. A third article, on the sects and schools of Buddhism, was never completed. Early in 1964 I was asked to write the chapter on Buddhism for the new edition of *The Legacy of India* and later that same year, having written my chapter, I left Kalimpong for England, which I had not seen for twenty years. The visit was to have lasted four months. Instead it lasted more than two years and eventually resulted in a permanent change of domicile, from India to England. It also resulted in a change of direction in my own life and in the lives of many other people.

Only in 1972, when it had been put aside for ten years, was I able to resume work on my autobiography. By that time I had founded the FWBO and WBO and was living in a flat at Muswell Hill. Though continuing to grow, the FWBO was homeless at the time, and for several months I had fewer classes to take than usual and could devote more time to writing. Not that I found it easy to reconnect with the autobiography. A lot had happened to me in the interim, and the man who took it up again in London in 1972 was in some respects a very different person from the man who put it aside in Kalimpong in 1962. I was also farther away by ten years from the period about which I had last written, and laboured, moreover, under the disadvantage of having to reconnect with the work right in the middle of a chapter—the chapter entitled 'The Three Lawyers'. But reconnect I did, and in the course of the summer produced about 25,000 words. 1973 was the year of my sabbatical. I spent most of it in a chalet on the coast of Cornwall, where I produced some 50,000 or so words more, and in 1976 *The Thousand-Petalled Lotus* appeared under the Heinemann imprint.

The title was not exactly of my own choosing. Or rather, it was not my *original* choice. My original choice, at least as a working title, was *The Rainbow Road*. The publishers did not like this; they asked me to think again; I submitted a list of five possible titles and from these they eventually selected 'The Thousand-Petalled Lotus'. They also insisted on my lopping off the first ten chapters of the book, dealing with my early life, on the grounds that this part of the story was of little or no general interest.

Strange to relate, more than one reviewer wondered why I had not written about my life prior to my arrival in Colombo at the end of 1944, while during the last fourteen years friends to whom the existence of the ten amputated chapters was known have increasingly urged me to have them published. This I am now doing—not entirely without misgivings. When, at Jivaka's suggestion, I started writing my autobiography I did so quite lightheartedly, without much regard either for the arrangement of my material or for literary style. Only after I had written quite a few tens of thousands of words did I realize the significance of what I was doing and start taking the work more seriously. For this reason the earlier chapters of the (original) *Thousand-Petalled Lotus* are, I think, less well written than some of the later ones—though here opinions may differ, an author being not necessarily the best judge of his own work. I also realized that I was not, in fact, writing my autobiography at all, that is, not writing my auto-biography: I was writing my *memoirs*. In the words of the unrevised version of the first of the ten amputated chapters the work on which I was engaged was 'less a collection of facts than an evocation of memories, from the degree of whose distinctness the more delicately percep-tive may gauge both the relative intensity of the experien-ces whose impressions they are and the nature and ultimate extent of the influence exerted by those experien-ces on the development of character and formation of opinion in the narrator.'

The lopping off of the first ten chapters of my memoirs naturally necessitated a few adjustments in the text of *The Thousand-Petalled Lotus* as published. These adjustments were of a minor character, and did not extend to the material now being brought out as *Learning to Walk*. In any case, that material had already been subjected to a fairly thorough revision in 1973. This was particularly the case with the first chapter, which was cut and rearranged to such an extent that I have decided to include the unrevised version as an appendix. I should also mention that the ten chapters now entitled *Learning to Walk* were typed for me in Kalimpong by Jivaka, and that in typing them he exer-cised his blue pencil pretty freely on what he termed my 'book lists', that is, my rather lengthy accounts of my reading. Fortunately or unfortunately, these accounts are no longer recoverable.

It only remains for me to thank Sue Lawson for typing the manuscript, Joyce Mumford for reading the proofs, and Shantavira and Nagabodhi for overseeing production, and to hope that the friends who have been urging me to have these recollections of my early life published will not be disappointed when they read them.

Sangharakshita
Sukhavati
London
20 May 1990

1. Giants And Dragons

On Sunday mornings, when the weather was fine, Father used to take me to see my grandmother, pushing the perambulator with the cream-coloured silk awning through two or three miles of south-west London streets.

As soon as he had swung open the front gate I used to run up the path and rattle the shining brass letterbox until someone come to let us in, all the time peering eagerly through the coloured glass panels of the big green front door. The hall never failed to interest me, and never did I pass through it without pausing to look up at the Nepalese kukris and Chinese swords and chopstick-sets with which the walls were decorated, and rarely could I refrain from ringing the Tibetan ritual handbell which stood in a corner behind the door.

What most of all drew my attention was the big Chinese picture on the left-hand wall. This Father had lifted me up to look at ever since I was a baby and it was thus among the most familiar objects of my childhood. Almost square in shape, it depicted an august and mysterious personage seated cross-legged on a kind of throne. He was arrayed in loosely flowing robes and behind his head was a nimbus. His features, which were markedly oriental, with slant almond eyes that gazed into the far distance, were expressive of a remarkable combination of benignity and power. This enigmatic being was surrounded by half a dozen figures, some making offerings, others playing on musical instruments. None of them was more than a tenth of the size of their master, whom for this reason I called the Giant.

Running into the sitting-room, I found objects to gaze at, and even to handle, which were hardly less wonderful than those in the hall. The Chinese cloisonné vases were as fine as any of those which, in later years, I saw in Tibetan temples and at the houses of wealthy Chinese friends, and the exquisite shape of some of them has been in my experience unique. One great flagon-shaped pair with gold dragon handles depicted houses, gardens, and human figures. Even now, at a distance of more than forty years, I can still see a favourite figure in blue gown and black cap standing pensively among the toy hills.

Round each of the other vases, all of which were a deep rich blue, coiled a five-clawed imperial dragon with white beard and tusks, red horns, black eyes, purple mane, and scales picked out in gold. Each dragon had its jewel and spat flame in its defence. Of these mysterious beasts it never occurred to me to feel afraid, and certainly they were never for me, as they are for the Christian tradition, symbolical of evil. It was therefore without astonishment that I leaned, in later life, that to the Chinese the dragon had been for thousands of years the symbol of the Yang, the bright, masculine, creative principle of the universe, even as the phoenix, with which I was unacquainted, was the symbol of the Yin, the dark, feminine, destructive principle.

On the mantelpiece was a small sedent bronze image which, when able to talk, I learned to call the Empress Dowager. When I shook it, it rattled. This figure, the features of which I remember as well as those of any living face, I now know represented not the last Manchu ruler of imperial China but the 'Goddess of Mercy', Kwan Yin, the feminized Chinese version of the Bodhisattva Avalokiteshvara, one of the most popular figures of the Indian Buddhist pantheon. The rattling noise must have been produced not, as I then supposed, by a stone, but by one of those holy relics which the Buddhists of China, like those of Tibet, frequently sealed in images.

In grandmother's kitchen there hung, on opposite walls, the portraits of two men, one in naval the other in military uniform. The man in the first, which was considerably larger, wore a walrus moustache and must have been about thirty. The man in the second picture, which was slightly yellowed, had a small trim moustache and seemed to be in his early twenties. At that time it puzzled me very much to be told that both men were my grandfather, for Nana, as we called her, had been twice married and twice widowed. By each marriage she had had two children, a boy and a girl, Father being the eldest. It was her second husband who was responsible for introducing into the house the exotic objects described. Of partly Portuguese descent, he had travelled widely, at one time serving in the Merchant Navy. At the time of the Boxer Rebellion he was working for the Imperial Chinese Government on the construction of railways and, having a mania for curios, took advantage of the sack of the Summer Palace at Pekin to add to his collection.

Grandfather was also a photographer, it seems, for there was an album of photographs taken at the time of the rebellion. Kneeling on the ground, hands pinioned behind their backs, were rows of naked rebels, some with their severed heads already at the executioner's feet. My sister spent many happy hours looking at these pictures, until one day Nana realized that they were not the most suitable thing for children to see.

About Nana's first husband, my own grandfather, I knew even less than I did about her second. This was partly because he had died so young that Father had no recollections of him to share with me. All I knew was that he came of a good Suffolk family, being the youngest of eight brothers, and that after their marriage he and Nana, the daughter of a Norfolk smallholder, had gone to live at Woolwich, where Father was born. Grandfather was then working in the War Office, on account of his fine copper-plate hand being assigned the responsibility of writing out the commissions that went to the Queen for signature. On his sudden death from pneumonia Nana was left to support herself and two small children, one of them still a baby. Being a woman of great strength of character she met the situation courageously and from odd reminiscences of hers in later years I gathered that at different times she had worked as charwoman, parlour-maid, and housekeeper. After five or six years of this hard life she had married again and come to live in Tooting.

Between Father and his sister, who was also my god-mother, existed a very strong affinity. Besides inheriting Nana's heavy eyebrows, blue-grey eyes, and aquiline nose, both of them were, like her, outspoken in opinion and firm in adherence to principle. But whereas Auntie Noni was exceptionally self-possessed, and could make the deadliest remarks with the utmost coolness, Father was hot-tempered in the extreme and almost morbidly quick to take offence. Since he was of a generous and forgiving nature his anger never lasted long, however, and by the time I was born his temper was more or less under control. Indeed he was an unusually good man. Unselfishness was second nature to him, and it was long before I met anyone who so consistently and so cheerfully put the happiness of others before his own. Auntie Noni, who was unmarried, idolized him. This was perhaps natural. Unfortunately, she was also in the habit of singing his praises to Mother and reminding her, on every possible occasion, what a good man Father was and how lucky she was to have married him. This last remark was always conveyed in a tone which suggested that having such a man for a husband was a miracle for which Mother ought to go down on her unworthy knees and render thanks to heaven.

Unlike Mother, both Father and Auntie Noni had a very lively sense of humour and were excellent raconteurs. Father's stories, which he told me when I had been put to bed, were usually about his own life, especially his school-days and his experiences in the trenches during the Great War. In this way I learned how he had given a false age in order to enlist, how he had lived under shellfire, and how he had seen comrades blown to bits and had been himself badly wounded, as well as how he had woken up in a hospital tent without the use of his right arm, which was permanently disabled. While convalescing in the Church Lane Hospital, Upper Tooting, he met Mother, who was working there as a V.A.D. One of his more amusing stories was about her helping him clamber over the hospital wall at night when he had stayed out after hours. They were married in 1919, when Father was nineteen and Mother perhaps twenty. Six years later, in a nursing home in Stockwell only a stone's throw from the spot where the English Buddhist monk Ananda Maitreya had died two years earlier, I was born.

At the time of my birth my parents were living in Nana's house in Tooting, where they occupied the upstairs flat. They had moved there some years earlier when, on the death of her second husband, Nana had shifted to South-fields. Brick-walled and slate-roofed, with a dusty privet hedge, lace-curtained windows, and highly polished front door, this modest terrace property was one of the hundreds of thousands which, standing back to back in interminable rows, help to make up the vast maze of mutually intersecting streets which is suburban London.

What I take to be my earliest memory, however, finds me not outside the house but inside it, in my parents' bedroom. Lying at night in the big double bed, where I had been put to sleep, I used to stare up at the foliated stucco ceiling-piece, the size and shape of a cartwheel, from the centre of which depended the unlit gas-bracket. As the motors passed up and down the main road at the top of the street their headlights swung round the ceiling-piece like great bright spokes round a shadowy hub. If the motors were going south, towards the coast, the spokes swung clockwise; if north, to the city's heart, in the opposite direction. With the clanging of distant tram-bells and the low roar and rumble of the other traffic in my ears, I used to lie in the darkness and watch the spokes turning now this way, now that, and now both ways simultaneously as two motors crossed each other, until lulled to sleep.

As I grew older I naturally became dissatisfied with passive contemplation. 'Mother, can I go out to play?' was my constant cry. The natural playground of the London child is, of course, the street, but there I was not allowed to play until after I had started school. In the meantime, therefore, I played on the black and white tiles of the porch and behind the dusty privet with my sister Joan, fifteen months younger than myself, and a girl of my own age who lived up the street. Sometimes we played so noisily that 'the lady downstairs' had to tap gently on the window of her front room to quieten us. When it rained, or when I was not allowed to play 'out in the front', my refrain was, 'Mother, can Frances come in to play?' Usually she could. Our favourite indoor game was 'dressing up', for which we ransacked the house for old lace curtains. As a special treat we were sometimes allowed to borrow the embroidered veil in which Father and I had been christened, and then great was our joy, for instead of playing mothers and fathers, as we usually did, we could play at weddings. In my case this love of dressing up persisted much longer than it did with the girls, and even at the age of eight I could spend hours in front of the wardrobe mirror experimenting with different styles of dress. Jersey and knickerbockers were not my real costume, I felt, and almost desperately I swathed and draped myself in lengths of material, searching in vain for my true vesture. The only times I felt satisfied was when, with the help of a Red Ensign, I achieved a toga-like effect which, though not exactly right, was to some extent what I desired. Gravely holding grandfather's silver-mounted amber cane, I would then stand gazing at my reflection with solemn pleasure.

Half-way up the street, on the other side of the road, stood the school Father had attended as a boy and to which, at the age of four, I too was sent. Ever since I could remember I had seen its turquoise green cupolas against the sky, and heard its bell ringing twice a day. Nevertheless, on the day of my admission I was so frightened that I ran home at the first opportunity. This reluctance to study did not last long and I spent in the Infants' Department four not unhappy years—the longest period of continuous schooling I was ever to receive.

After tea on weekdays, all day Saturday (though not usually on Sunday), as well as practically every day during the holidays, we were free to play in the street. Frances, Joan, and I continued to share our games, for though we knew many other children we formed a self-contained little confederacy and were happiest playing with one another. We never played all our games on one day. As I look back it seems that our games had their cycles and that conkers and marbles, spinning-tops and hopscotch, came and went in accordance with laws as immutable as those of physics or chemistry. On or about a certain day in August, for example, all the children in the neighbourhood would begin making grottoes, any attempt to set them up earlier, or to prolong their existence for more than three weeks, being regarded as extremely reprehensible. These grottoes, which were always built on the pavement against a wall, consisted of shells or small stones arranged in the form of a square, within which could be set flowers, small pieces of crockery and any bright or curious object. After constructing the grottoes we had the right to sit by them and demand coppers from the passers-by.

Another event that loomed large in our year was Derby Day, when throughout the afternoon and evening and until late at night a continuous stream of cars, buses, coaches, and horsedrawn carts and carriages, all packed with happy and excited racegoers, would be flowing past the top of the street along the main road between London and Epsom. Waving red, white, and blue streamers, swarms of excited children would be standing on the kerb, their parents generally hovering behind to see that they did not fall under the wheels of the vehicles. When, races over and bets lost and won, the stream of traffic set more and more steadily in the homeward direction, our excitement reached its climax. Each brightly lit coach that swung slowly past us would be greeted by a shout of 'Throw out yer mouldies!' whereupon the beerily jovial occupants would fling into our midst handfuls of coppers for which we scrambled and fought until the next coach came along. At intervals, with the crack of a whip and the jingle of beribboned harness, there would pass by, in all the glory of innumerable gleaming pearl buttons, a Pearly King and Pearly Queen. They were always stout and elderly, while the Queen, who was generally stouter than the King and laughed with even greater heartiness, invariably wore a wide black hat with enormous ostrich plumes that nodded and danced at every step the pony took.

Yet another annual event was Guy Fawkes' Day. As soon as it was dark, Joan and I, Mother and Father, and sometimes Nana and Auntie Noni too, would file downstairs into our tiny back yard where the guy had already been propped up in the middle of the concrete. After Father had sprinkled him with petrol he was set on fire, whereupon the flames would leap up, the smoke swirl, and the darkness be lit up with a ruddy glare in which our faces would glow crimson and our voices sound strangely different. Sparklers, which we could run about with in our hands, and Roman Candles and Golden Rain, which had to be set at a distance on the ground, would then be ignited. Catherine wheels would go whizzing round, broadcasting a shower of rainbow sparks, and red and green rockets spring hissing up into the night. Squibs and crackers exploded at our feet. In less than half an hour our Guy Fawkes would be blazing merrily. Ten more minutes and its head, charred features no longer recognizable, would collapse into the flames, sending up a shower of orange-gold sparks. Within the hour the bonfire would have burned itself out and the last flames have subsided, leaving only a mass of glowing embers. Standing silent in the darkness, our shouts and laughter hushed, we would look up through the misty air and see that the stars had come out in the chill November sky.

To what extent London children keep up the old customs, or are familiar with the traditional sights and sounds, I do not know. Perhaps they still hear the muffin-bell in the distance, still see the knife-grinder pushing his grinding-wheel through narrow suburban streets and the rag-and-bone man offering tortoises and goldfish in exchange for scrap iron, old clothes, old newspapers, and broken china. But I am sure none of them ever saw the lamplighter on his rounds. Even before we left the house at Tooting the old gas streetlights, which on rainy days were reflected in a strange iridescence from the wet pavements, had been replaced by electric standards. As late as eight o'clock at the height of summer and as early as four o'clock in the depths of winter, the old lamplighter would come down the street. Having set his ladder against the arm of the lamp-post he would climb up, open the window of the glass shade, light the mantle, adjust the flame and climb down, shoulder his ladder and be off down the street to the next lamp-post. I am sure there is hardly anything lonelier in the world than a deserted street in a big city, dimly lit at intervals by gas lamps.

Not that Joan and I were ever allowed out alone after dark. But sometimes in the summer, when it was fully light at six o'clock, Mother would send us to the Broadway to meet Father. Tooting Broadway, where the statue of Edward VII in royal robes dominated the public conveniences from its marble pedestal, and where the trams lumbered past with a dreadful grinding of wheels and shrieking of brakes, was to us the hub of the universe. It was, indeed, one of the biggest traffic junctions and busiest shopping centres in South London, though Father could remember how, at the beginning of the century, the High Street had been a country road with green fields on either side. Waiting inside the vestibule of the Tube, Joan and I used to feast our eyes on the gilded baskets of colourful hot-house fruits hanging in the windows of Walton's the Fruiterers. Every time a blast of hot air struck us from the escalator shaft, which meant a train had come in, we craned eagerly forward, searching for Father among the crowd pouring through the gate. As soon as we saw him, bareheaded and attaché case in hand, coming towards us with his rolling, rather nautical stride, we would dash forward and, seizing hold of a hand apiece, lead him home in triumph.

Once in the kitchen, I would open his case and take out the newspaper, which was always the *Daily Herald*, for unlike the rest of the family Father was a staunch supporter of the Labour Party. His only concession to conservatism was to take the *Sunday Express*, a paper Nana also read. Later on, I do not know why, he changed to the *People*. My own interest in the *Daily Herald*, which I read spread out on the floor, it being too big for me to hold at arm's length, was strictly non-political. I was interested in following the adventures of Bobby Bear. Only after informing myself of the latest exploits of this hero did I turn to the news. It was from Father's newspaper, I think, rather than from any school primer, that I learned to read.

The first real book I ever handled was the family Bible, with its tooled leather cover and worn gilt clasp, which was so big and heavy that I could hardly lift it. Imitating Father, I call it 'Grandmother's Bible', the volume having formerly belonged to Nana's mother, who was, however, still living, and whom I saw only once. The rich blues, reds, and yellows of the illustrations, which depicted such subjects as Daniel kneeling in the lions' den among skulls and ribs and Samson with the ass's jawbone in his hand, had long been familiar to me. One rainy day, when I was five or six years old, it occurred to me that instead of merely looking at the pictures I could read the text, whereupon I promptly spelled my way through the first and second chapters of Genesis.

If the Bible gave me my first experience of prose, it was from a prayer book that I had my first taste of poetry. In the sitting-room cupboard, among Father's books, I discovered at the age of six or seven a volume entitled *Prayer and Praise at Eventide*. From the inscription on the fly leaf I gathered that it had been presented to my paternal grandfather by his mother. Opening it, I came on the lines

> *Stay, pilgrim, stay!*
> *Night treads upon the heels of the day.*

This was the first time I had ever met a metaphor and I can still recall the shock of delight the experience gave me. Though I read the rest of the volume, even the prayers, none of it had for me the magic of those two lines.

Nana visited us once a week on the day she came from Southfields to Tooting to see her old friends, collect her rents, and do a little shopping. Auntie Noni came less often. With the exception of Father's friends and their wives, nearly all the other visitors were Mother's relations. The most frequent and regular of these were Auntie Kate and Auntie Jessie.

Only the creator of the Aunts in *The Mill on the Floss* could have done them justice, though neither of them had either the formidability of Aunt Glegg or the airs and graces of Aunt Dean. Auntie Kate, who could not quite be called stout, had a watery blue eye with a twinkle in it and wore her hair in a bun kept in position by large hairpins. Her nose, which being the family nose could only be called long, was red at the end and shiny, for despite the expostulations of Mother and Auntie Jessie she refused to powder. Their epithet for her was 'old-fashioned', which was hardly matter for astonishment since she was the eldest of the sisters and had already married and given birth to a son when Mother, who was the youngest, was still in the cradle. Auntie Kate was in fact an old-timer in many ways. Even the sweets she brought us were of a kind that must have been on the market in Dickensian times. Her sense of humour, too, was nineteenth century, and when on holiday at the seaside she used to send all her friends and relations comic postcards depicting enormously fat women in bathing costumes and with exaggeratedly prominent posteriors. Yet Auntie Kate was a victim of melancholia, and in later years used to spend her evenings reading *Jack the Ripper*, after which she would put out the light and sit alone in the dark.

Auntie Jessie's epithet was 'stately', even as Mother's was 'vivacious'. She had a full bosom, kind brown eyes, a musical voice, and was always redolent of scent and powder. Moreover she was quiet and gentle, with a touch of sadness in her expression. Unlike Auntie Kate she relished a ribald joke well enough to laugh at one but not well enough to tell one, and while laughing she always put her hand up to her mouth as if to hide a blush or her rather prominent false teeth.

On visiting days the two aunts usually arrived early in the afternoon; but sometimes they came at eleven o'clock, on which occasions Auntie Kate would scandalize Mother and Auntie Jessie by producing her own lunch, cold meat and pickled onions, out of a brown paper bag. After discussing haberdashery and husbands, and drinking innumerable cups of tea, the three sisters would try on one another's hats, for they all frequently bought new ones, and at each meeting at least one hat was produced which at least one sister had not seen. This ritual accomplished, Auntie Kate and Auntie Jessie would pull on their gloves, pick up their handbags and, after kisses all round, depart to catch the tram home.

At that period Auntie Kate lived, as indeed she had always lived, at Fulham, and twice or thrice a year Mother and I visited her there. As we crossed over Wandsworth Bridge and passed the rows of meanly decent houses where, at six o'clock on a cold December night, one might well be tempted to murmur

The winter evening settles down
With smell of steaks in passageways,

Mother would point out to me one house, bigger than the rest, which held a special place in her affections. This was the house where she had been born. Sometimes the sight of the old home revived memories, and then Mother would tell me about the grandfather who had been born in Hungary and could speak only a little broken English and in whose sweetshop she used to help as a girl, and about the father who had been a clarinettist and whom she had sometimes accompanied to recitals on the Continent. She also talked about her brothers and sisters, thirteen in number, not all of whom I had seen. Uncle Dick, the youngest, who like his father was a clarinettist, had gone to India at the age of sixteen and joined the Governor of Bengal's band. This brother was the innocent cause of one of the cruellest disappointments of my boyhood. When I was six he returned to England on leave. The news of his arrival threw me into a fever of excitement, for I assumed he would be accompanied by a whole retinue of Indian servants, and never having set eyes on an Indian before I looked forward to his coming to the house with the keenest anticipation. Alas! as the kitchen door opened, and I craned my head forward for a glimpse of the

Dusk faces with white silken turbans wreathed

which I hoped to see beaming over his shoulder, all I saw was the very European features of Uncle Dick, Auntie Dolly, and my two small cousins.

At Christmas time representatives of both Mother's and Father's families would be invited to the house, though Mother often complained that 'her side' was being neglected. Preparations for the festival began with the purchase of large quantities of holly and mistletoe from a barrow at Tooting Broadway, where the brightly lit shop windows already glittered with tinsel and where, during Christmas week, the slow-moving crowds of cheerful shoppers thronged the pavements more and more densely every night. The peak was the last Saturday before Christmas, when with the help of Nana's expert eye we bought the turkey, and when the last stir was given to the

Christmas pudding. In the kitchen and the sitting-room Father would put up paper chains, which we sometimes made ourselves from slips of coloured paper, as well as Chinese lanterns, bunches of balloons, and paper bells. There was also a Christmas tree, which we decorated with iridescent globes of coloured glass saved from year to year, candles of red, blue, green, and yellow wax, and strings of tinsel. The lower branches were hung with presents, while at the top of the tree glittered a large tinsel star.

On Christmas day itself, the first thing I did was to empty the stocking hanging at the foot of the bed and open the parcels heaped on a chair at my bedside. In the toe of the stocking there was always a tangerine. The remainder of the morning was spent in the sitting-room, where there were dishes of nuts and packets of figs and dates and where, at noon, Joan and I would be given a glass of port wine to drink with our mince pie. As the turkey had to be roasted for several hours, Christmas dinner was a late meal. Flushed and triumphant, Mother would emerge from the scullery amidst clouds of steam bearing the turkey—a sprig of holly stuck in its breast—before her on a large oval dish. After dinner presents were untied from the tree and distributed. In the evening Father sometimes played his favourite gramophone records, among which I remember an operatic aria sung by Caruso, of whom he was very fond, and Gershwin's *Rhapsody in Blue*. From the way in which the clarinet climbed the scale in the opening bars of the latter piece I called it 'the aeroplane'.

Birthdays were celebrated in much the same way, though on a considerably reduced scale, turkey and Christmas pudding being replaced by a birthday cake with the appropriate number of candles, while instead of an assembly of grown-ups there would be a small gathering of children. But for me Christmases and birthdays alike always ended in disaster, for I would get keyed up to such

a pitch of excitement that, however tired, I could not bear the thought of going to bed. The result was that Father had to exert his authority and send me off to my own room in tears. Even so early in life did I have to learn that
Every sweet with sour is tempered still.

2. The Children's Encyclopaedia

One cold bright December morning, when I was eight years old, I opened my pyjama jacket, pulled my vest up to my chin, and stood on a chair in front of the window so that the doctor could peer more closely at my chest. It was covered with dull red spots. Making me turn round he scrutinized my back. The same dull red spots! 'Scarlet fever,' he said briefly. 'He'll have to go to hospital.'

Though I had had measles and whooping cough, as well as influenza, this was the first time it had been necessary for me to be removed to hospital, and I was filled with apprehension. Besides, it was only a week before Christmas, and I was deeply disturbed by the prospect of missing any of the customary festivities. To assuage my fears, a copy of *Alice in Wonderland* was taken prematurely from its hiding-place in a cupboard with the assurance that, if I was a good boy and went to the hospital without making a fuss, I would definitely be home in time to open the rest of my presents on Christmas morning. When the ambulance arrived, therefore, I left quite cheerfully, clutching the *Alice in Wonderland* and declaring loudly that I would be back in four or five days.

Perhaps I would not have gone so quietly had I known that I should be away for five weeks and that, even when I did eventually return, it would be to an existence quite different from the one to which I was accustomed, and that

I should be allowed no festivities of any sort for several years.

The ward where I found myself in bed an hour later contained about forty boys of different ages, all with scarlet fever. At first I took refuge behind the *Alice in Wonderland*, now my sole memento of home. But soon my nervousness abated, I became used to the disciplined routine of hospital life and started making friends with some of the other boys. Our day began very early. Long before the short winter day had dawned two cheery cleaners, clad in pink gowns and white aprons, would clatter in with mops and pails and proceed to swing the castored truckle beds out into the centre of the ward with a single heave of their brawny arms. When they had swept, scrubbed, dusted, and polished every square inch of wood and metal, so that wood shone like glass and metal gleamed like silver and gold, beds would be pushed into position against the wall and the patients given their breakfast. Having never been interested in food, I remember of the hospital meals only the unpleasant thickness of the china mugs from which we drank our well-diluted milk. Breakfast finished, faces and hands were washed, ear-passages and nostrils cleaned. Finally, our beds were made, the coarse white sheets being turned back half way down the bed and tucked in so tightly that the mattress curved like a bow.

Christmas morning found me eagerly untying the parcel Father had left in the hall the night before. Though it contained all manner of good things, including books and toys, I remember best of all the two sour red plums he had tucked into a corner of the box. In spite of our protests, and even tears, we were not allowed to keep our presents, all of which went into the common toy-box in the bathroom.

While the cheerful faces and friendly voices of the two cleaners are still vivid in my mind, of the nurses, with the exception of the ward sister, I remember nothing. They were, as no doubt they had been trained to be, machines for taking temperatures and administering medicines, though human hearts must have beaten somewhere beneath those starched bosoms. The ward sister was very pretty, and severe almost to the point of spitefulness. She it was who, every evening before we went to sleep, pencil in hand, and with the face of a Medusa, held an investigation into the state of our bowels during the day, giving a tick in the register if they had moved and a zero and a glass of syrup of senna if they had not. Constipation, we were made to feel, was a criminal offence. On one occasion, when I had tremblingly admitted for the third day in succession that I had had no motion, she scolded me harshly and told me to go to the lavatory and sit there until my recalcitrant bowels had moved.

Fortunately not all my hospital experiences were as unpleasant. On my return from the chickenpox ward, where I was isolated for a week with three or four other boys, I was allowed to spend most of the day out of bed. One morning the other convalescent boys and I were taken downstairs into the courtyard where we played for an hour in the pallid brightness of the winter sunshine under the guardianship of the oldest patient, a lad of twelve. When confined to the ward we amused ourselves sliding up and down the highly polished floor in our stockinged feet. But my pleasantest memory is of the hours we spent singing together 'Underneath the Arches', 'Shanty Town', and the rest of the Flanagan and Allen songs, then at the height of their popularity.

While I was in hospital only one boy died. We had been aware for several days that he was more seriously ill than other patients, for when the doctors came screens were placed around his bed, and once to our horror we saw several yards of rubber piping disappearing behind the green curtains of the screens. One day two figures, muffled in red cloaks and hoods, came and sat with him for an hour. That night, when only a dim blue light burned in the ward, and the night sister sat writing at the table, I saw shadowy figures flitting between his bed and the door. They seemed to be carrying something heavy. In the morning, when the screens were dismantled, we saw that the boy was no longer there.

On the day of my discharge one of the nurses took Mother aside and told her that my exceptionally high pulse-rate, which had always been attributed to my well-known fear of doctors, might be due to some other cause. She advised her to take me to our own doctor and have my heart thoroughly tested. Alarmed, my parents had this done without delay, and it was discovered that I apparently had valvular disease of the heart. Years later there was considerable controversy between medical men over the cause of my complaint. According to some of them it was due to my having had rheumatic fever in very early childhood. Our own doctor, however, to whom I had been taken for every cough and cold since I was born, maintained that I had never had rheumatic fever. In my own opinion the disease was functional, that is, of psychological origin. After I went to India and took up the practice of Buddhist meditation, which calms the mind and helps resolve complexes, there was a marked improvement in my condition.

Whatever the origin of the disease might have been, about the way in which it was to be treated the general practitioner had in those days no doubts. I was ordered to bed, where I had to remain flat on my back. Thenceforward I saw only the nasturtium-patterned walls of my room where, hour after hour for two years, I watched the eyes of the owl clock moving backwards and forwards with a sharp click-clack as the pendulum swung to and fro.

Since I had to be kept absolutely quiet, no visitors were admitted. I saw only the doctor, who at the beginning came thrice a day, the district nurse, and my parents. Once Joan, finding the door open, peeped in with a scared face. A few months prior to my catching scarlet fever I had been promoted to the Junior Department at school and my teacher, a red-faced, kindhearted little woman, unwilling to suffer my education to be discontinued, offered to teach me spelling and arithmetic in her spare time. But when it was found that these lessons agitated me they were stopped.

During the whole period of my confinement my parents were continually occupied by two problems: how to keep me quiet and how to keep me occupied. The first problem, the solution of which was the more urgent, inasmuch as my life was thought to depend on it, could be solved by such measures as not allowing me ever to sit up in bed by my own exertions, and by excluding visitors and shutting out noise. The second, it was soon discovered, could be solved by providing me with books and magazines, and I promptly developed a habit of avid and incessant reading which never afterwards left me.

Soon after my incarceration began, Father brought into my room an armful of books from his own library and arranged them in the little bookcase on the wall, on top of which stood the model yacht *White Eagle* given me by Nana for my seventh birthday. Some of Father's books I had already read. In addition to *An Outline of English Church History* and a pocket *Johnson's Dictionary*, both of which like *Prayer and Praise at Eventide* had belonged to my grandfather, there were Harrison Ainsworth's *The Tower of London*, E.W. Hornung's *Raffles*, Walter Besant's *The World Went Very Well Then*, *Peter the Whaler*, *Tom Brown's Schooldays*, Kingsley's *Hypatia*, Charlotte Brontë's *Jane Eyre*, and an illustrated English Reader, beside others now forgotten. This odd collection of books, every one of which I read and re-read, laid the foundations of my education, for neither before nor after my illness was I able to learn at school anything that could be considered either useful or interesting.

Like the baby cuckoo which keeps its sparrow foster-parents flying to and fro all day with food for its insatiable maw, I gave my parents no respite from the search for reading matter. Immediately after breakfast Father would dash round the corner to the newsagent's and bring me back a boy's weekly, one of which was published every day. My favourite was the *Wizard*, published on Monday, with the *Adventurer*, *Hotspur*, and *Rover* following not far behind. The *Champion*, which appeared on Thursday, stood low in favour, for it consisted mainly of stories with a sporting background, while the famous *Gem* and *Magnet*, which contained nothing but rather silly stories about boys in Eton jackets and masters in billowing gowns (the gowns always 'billowed' in these stories), I considered not worth reading. My preference was for the exotic. The indefatigable writers who, week after week, turned out the latest enthralling instalment of the serials which I followed with so much interest, catered for the natural boyish craving for adventure by exploiting three distant parts of the globe—Darkest Africa (tom-toms and cannibalism), the Wild West (cattle-rustling and scalping), and the Mysterious East (tongs, opium-fiends, six-inch fingernails, and throwing-hatchets). One serial, however, had a Dyak head-hunter for hero, while in another Tibetan lamas in tall hoods, and with steel-devouring termites concealed in the seams of their robes, came to England and gained hypnotic control over a champion football team as a means of raising money for their government.

Of all the stories it was the ones about the Mysterious East that most excited my interest and stimulated my imagination, and I had not been many months in bed when I wrote a story of my own set in the same opium-laden atmosphere of warring tongs and international smuggling rings, where fatal hatchets suddenly flashed through the air from silken sleeves, and men who had talked were dragged out of the river by the police. This story was my first literary effort. No doubt Father read it, and perhaps he thought that vicarious escapes from sudden and violent death were not the best thing for valvular disease of the heart, and I did no more writing.

Out of the dozen or so books he had given me, my greatest favourites were *Jane Eyre* and *Hypatia*. I can still see the narrow black figure of Mr Brocklehurst astride Mrs Reed's hearthrug, still hear him ordering Jane's naturally curly hair to be shorn as a rebuke to worldly vanity, after which awful sentence his wife and daughters (exquisite satire!) come rustling into the room in all the splendour of their silk and satin and glory of false fronts and flowing ringlets. No less vividly do I remember the haughty Miss Blanche at the piano, Mr Rochester making his unconventional declaration, and the mad wife escaping from her chamber at midnight to rend Jane's bridal veil. In fact almost every incident in this extraordinary novel, which ten years later I could still read with enjoyment, is printed indelibly on my mind.

Much less vivid is *Hypatia*, which as literature merely flutters its wings where *Jane Eyre* soars with ease, though strong impressions of this tale of the best of Paganism and the worst of Christianity in naked conflict still remain. My sympathies were very much with the last of the Neoplatonists, and I was unspeakably shocked when the Christian mob, incited by Cyril the archbishop, tore her to pieces on the altar-steps of the great basilica beneath the very eyes of Christ. But even more deeply than by this tragic incident was I impressed by Hypatia's address to her students, in the course of which I heard for the first time the thunder-roll of Homeric verse, and by the description of her lying rigid upon her couch while her soul flew alone to the Alone. This was my first acquaintance with mystical religion and was never to be forgotten.

Religion in any form had not, indeed, occupied a very prominent place in my early life. Though baptized soon after birth into the Church of England, to which Father's family belonged, I had never been made to comply with any form of religious observance. For a short while Joan and I attended Sunday School at the nearby Congregational Church, sitting on a hard bench against the wall in the bottom class and feeling extremely bored. More interesting was my first service, from which I returned to tell my parents that I had seen the Holy Ghost. Enquiry revealed that this phenomenon was in fact the minister, who had appeared in a white surplice.

My parents' indifference to religious observances was due, I think, not so much to any deficiency of religious instinct on their part as to the lifeless formalism which seemed to have blighted all the churches, chapels, tabernacles, and meeting houses of Tooting. The only sign of spiritual life to be discerned in our neighbourhood were the grey-haired Salvation Army lasses who, in poke bonnets and with banners bearing such legends as 'JESUS DIED FOR YOU', stood under the leadership of an aged captain outside the Trafalgar every Sunday morning and in cracked voices sang doleful hymns to the squeak of a concertina and the rattle of tambourines. Father always gave them a copper, for though, like most Londoners, he could not agree with their religious opinions, he respected them for their integrity and for the nobility of their social work.

Only once do I remember seeing a clergyman in the street. This was the Congregational minister, who, like

Mr Chadband, wore black and was a fat yellow man who looked as though he had a good deal of train oil in his system. Probably this clerical elusiveness helped give me the feeling which, during the present century, has become almost universal in Protestant countries, that religion is the business of the clergy and that its manifestations are confined in space to the Churches and in time to Sunday mornings and evenings. At any rate, no clergyman was ever known to visit the house, and only after removal to another part of Tooting did we become the object of ministerial solicitude.

When orthodoxy decays heterodoxy flourishes, and in the absence of more solid spiritual nourishment Father turned to the Ancient and Mystical Order of Druids, of which he became a member, and to Dr Coué's New Thought, while Mother turned to the Rechabites. My first experience of a religious gathering took place under the auspices of this obscure sect, whose principal tenet was teetotalism. I accompanied Mother to a meeting at the suggestion of one of her friends, the mother of a classmate of mine, who said, 'Oh, Gerald simply *loves* Rechabites!'. I did not love them. All they did was to sit gloomily around a table in a small room in Balham while an elderly man read aloud from a black Bible, after which they drank cups of strong tea. Perhaps they said prayers too, but I do not remember any. Mother was probably as dissatisfied as I was, for she soon stopped going. When I was older she dabbled in Spiritualism and attended séances with a friend. Later she joined the Baptist Church at Streatham, which for a time occupied an important place in my own religious life, and still later, under her son's guidance, she became mildly interested in Buddhism.

Beneath these changes in religious affiliation her basic attitude remained unaltered. Nothing that anyone was reported to have said or done, however wicked, ever roused her indignation or made her feel, even when she had herself been wronged, that they should be punished by human hand. In her opinion the consequences of one's actions were inescapable, and he who did evil inevitably suffered. At the same time she never alluded to God, whom one born a Christian might be expected to regard as a rewarder of good and punisher of evil, from which I conclude that she believed in a principle not unlike the Buddhist karma, according to which pleasant and painful sensations arise in natural dependence upon pure and impure mental states respectively without the intervention of any external agency.

Having nothing to do except read, the rapidity with which I could devour a book became quite alarming: I must have held the world record for a boy of my age. How many words one issue of the *Wizard* or *Hotspur* contained I no longer recollect, but I remember boasting to Father, who had fondly imagined that one of them sufficed me for a whole day, that it had lasted twenty-five minutes exactly by the owl clock. Instead of being pleased with my precocity he looked dismayed. It was rather as though the baby cuckoo, after swallowing a particularly fat and juicy worm, which its overworked foster parents had thought would satisfy its demands for the day, should immediately open its beak and declare it was still hungry. Fortunately the problem was solved by the next-door neighbours. This kindhearted couple, a printer and his wife, who had passed their *Everybody's* over the fence to us every week for several years, now gave me a complete set, in sixty-one parts, of Harmsworth's *Children's Encyclopaedia*. This was a sizeable morsel even for a digestion like mine, and it kept me fairly quiet for the remainder of the two years.

Edward Harmsworth, afterwards Lord Northcliffe, has sometimes been ridiculed on account of his enthusiasm for popular education; but I fervently blessed him for the *Children's Encyclopaedia*. All sixty-one parts (including the Index) were at my bedside day and night, and rarely was I seen without one of them in my hand. Thanks to Mr Harmsworth I was no longer alone in my little room with the nasturtium-patterned wallpaper, the owl clock, the model yacht, and my one dozen oft-read volumes. I could now speak with the good and wise of all ages; I could follow Nature into her innermost recesses and explore all her secrets, from the constitution of the heavens to the structure of a crystal. The pageant of history from its first dawnings in Egypt, China, and Babylonia, passed with all its kings and princes, its priests and nobles and common people, before my eyes. The buskined and unbuskined heroes of ancient and modern tragedy trod my bedside rug for their stage. Perseus slew Medusa the Gorgon, Hercules performed his Twelve Labours, and Jason went in search of the Golden Fleece, in my sight. Shining presences of marble and bronze rose as though to music and stood before me in the naked glory of their perfectly proportioned Hellenic manhood; pensive Italian madonnas smiled. The cross on which Christ was crucified, the tree beneath which the Buddha attained enlightenment, had their roots in the floor of my room, wherein, as into a garner, the harvest of the ages was gathered unto me for the making of the bread that would keep my soul alive. The body was forgotten, and my imagination, now possessed of 'infinite riches in a little room', rejoiced in the freedom of all the heavens of the spirit.

Though not a page of those sixty-one parts remained unread, it was inevitable that some subjects should interest me more than others. My favourite sections, to which I turned most frequently, and over which I lingered longest, were the ones dealing with Art, with History, and with Literature—or rather, with the History of Literature, for the *Children's Encyclopaedia* being not a thesaurus of select classics but an outline of knowledge in all its branches, the only species of literature actually represented was Poetry, to which a separate section was devoted.

Strangely enough the Philosophy section, which discussed abstract ideas such as Truth, Beauty, Goodness, and Justice, all of which Mr Harmsworth had stoutly capitalized, failed to awaken in me the love of wisdom, though I studied with interest the lives of the great philosophers, as well as those of the Buddha, Mohammed, Zoroaster, Confucius, and Lao Tzu. Archaeology, however, fascinated me, especially that of Ancient Egypt, and I never wearied of looking at the picture of a pharoah with red-brown face in profile, his hair done up in slender braids, the double crown of Upper and Lower Egypt on his head, and the crook and flail, symbols of protection and punishment, crossed over his linen-clad breast; nor of gazing at those pages from the Book of the Dead, with their green Osiris and black-headed Anubis, or at the fresco of the fowler poised, sling in hand, upon his little boat among the reeds and lotuses, while the ducks flew up above his head.

The section which attracted me least was Popular Science, perhaps because I had no means of performing even the simplest of the experiments described. Neither was I particularly interested in the circulation of the blood or in the internal combustion engine. Perhaps at this period I was more strongly attracted by Beauty than by either Truth or Goodness. Certainly I was never tired of looking at what were to me the most precious parts of the whole Encyclopaedia—the numerous plates, some of them in full colour, which illustrated the history of Art, especially of painting and sculpture, in Ancient Greece and Rome, Italy, France, England, Germany, Spain, and Holland. Though every picture gave me pleasure, I admired most of all the works of the Renaissance artists, especially the deific sublimity of Michelangelo and the dancing delicacy of Botticelli.

Towards the end of the second year of my confinement my parents started giving even more serious thought to my condition than before. If I was no worse, neither was I noticeably any the better, and they could not help wondering whether I was doomed to lifelong invalidism, like white-faced Auntie Fanny at Besthorpe, who had not been outside her room for twenty years. In these circumstances it was only natural that they should feel the advisability of having a second medical opinion. Another doctor, therefore, was called in, and after examining me he confirmed our own physician's diagnosis and recommended continuation of the regimen already prescribed. Still dissatisfied, Father made arrangements for me to be examined by the famous heart specialist Dr Mackenzie. As he bore me into the consulting room, Dr Mackenzie asked, 'Why are you carrying him? Let him walk!'

'He can't walk,' explained Father, for to such a degree had I lost the use of my legs that I could not even stand.

'Can't walk!' roared the cardiologist, 'He must be *made* to walk! Put him down! Put him down!'

Whether his diagnosis agreed with that of the other doctors I have no knowledge. All I know is that he told Father in the strongest possible terms that I should be got out of bed immediately and allowed to run about. Twenty years later, in Calcutta, I met a Bengali doctor, also a heart specialist, who had studied under Dr Mackenzie. After hearing my story he told me that this great cardiologist had revolutionized the method of treating diseases of the heart and that after considerable initial opposition his findings had won general acceptance. At my Bengali friend's request I allowed him to examine my heart, which he pronounced perfectly sound.

When Dr Mackenzie gave his unexpected verdict, he was regarded as daringly, even dangerously, heterodox by the majority of the members of a profession which attaches as much importance to its own special form of orthodoxy as the most zealous religionists do to theirs. In this conflict of expert opinion Father had no means of judging who was right and who wrong. Eventually, after much anxious thought, he took the responsibility into his own hands and resolved to follow a middle course. No doubt this was a difficult decision, the making of which required not only common sense but courage; but in neither of these two qualities was Father at any time deficient. Mother, in her distress, consulted an occultist. Gazing into a crystal ball, he said that he saw me ascending a flight of golden stairs and disappearing over the top.

3. Learning to Walk

It was late spring when, wrapped in a blanket in Father's arms, I looked out of the scullery window down at his tiny garden. Though I did not see there Primavera in person, with Venus, Cupid, Flora, Zephyr, and the Three Graces, as in Botticelli's picture, the prospect could hardly have been more delightful if I had. Pansies and marigolds, stocks and antirrhinums, looked up at me from their built-up bed at the far end of the yard. On the wire netting to the right hung red and yellow nasturtiums and the tiny stars of the virginia creeper. To the left, surrounded by pieces of crazy paving, stood a small pond, the dark waters of which showed every now and then a red-gold gleam as a goldfish rose to the surface. From the aviary I could hear the chirp and twitter of the green budgerigars.

Thereafter, instead of lying in bed, I spent the day reclining on a bed-chair in the kitchen, where I once again saw Nana and Auntie Noni, Auntie Kate and Auntie Jessie, and other visitors.

The next step was to get me up and walking. Since two doctors were of opinion that if I attempted to stand I would immediately collapse, perhaps dying on the spot, this had to be managed with extreme caution. However, when at last I succeeded in standing on my own two feet I did not collapse. Instead, I sprained both ankles, since they were too weak to support me. Due to these sprains it was three weeks before I could renew the attempt; but renew it I did and eventually succeeded in standing, somewhat shakily, beside the bed-chair. As I seemed none the worse for the experiment, I was allowed to take a step or two. This I did clinging to the furniture and after a few weeks' practice could walk slowly across the room without much difficulty.

Seeing how pale my long confinement had made me, and being himself a great lover of the open air, Father bought an invalid chair and started taking me out in it on as many fine days as possible. Sometimes we went as far afield as Mitcham Common. On one such excursion, when Father was picking buttercups and cornflowers a short distance away, I saw a lizard sunning itself on the matted grass beneath a gorse-bush. Now I had always loved these little reptiles and before my illness had once or twice caught them on Wimbledon Common. The sight of this one, with his slim chocolate-brown body, cocked head, and beady eyes over which the thin secondary eyelid would every now and then be drawn, filled me with excitement. Forgetting my invalidism I leaped out of the chair and ran towards him. Father yelled a warning and rushed back, but by the time he reached me I was lying unconscious on the grass. This misadventure put me back into my room for several months, and when I emerged for the second time the whole procedure of standing up and learning to walk had to be repeated. Though our outings continued, and though I was permitted to walk about in the house, from that time onwards I could not so much as raise my hand quickly without an anxious voice immediately saying 'Be careful!' or 'Go slowly!'

As might have been foreseen, the intense love of Art which I had imbibed from the Art Section of the *Children's Encyclopaedia* developed, by a natural transition, from passive enjoyment to active creation, and when I was neither

being propelled over Mitcham Common by one parent nor
pushed around Tooting Broadway by the other I would
either draw or paint. My first drawing was an imaginary
head of Cleopatra, complete with uraeus; the second, King
George V in coronation robes. These were followed by
sketches of Queen Elizabeth I, one of my favourite characters in history, whom I often drew, and of Mary Queen of
Scots, both betraying the hand of the beginner in the face,
but very carefully executed as to ruffs and stomachers,
crowns and jewels. Early paintings included one of that
old friend of my childhood the Chinese dragon, rampant
in all the splendour of purple mane and crimson claw, an
Egyptian landscape showing palm trees against a sunset
on which I lavished all the reds and oranges and yellows
in my paintbox, and portraits of King Henry VIII and his
mother Elizabeth of York. These and other products of my
joint devotion to Art and History were shown to visitors
and duly admired and the feeling became general that I
was going to be an artist.

Despite his fear lest I should over-exert myself, Father
never forgot his hope that I would one day be able, if not
to leap and run, at least to walk like other boys. After a few
months of divided allegiance to Nature and Art, I was
allowed to spend more and more time on my feet and less
and less in the wheel-chair, which eventually could be
dispensed with altogether. I was even allowed to play in
the street. This welcome improvement in my condition
made a marked difference not to me only but to the whole
family. We could all go to Southfields on Sunday afternoons. Mother and I could continue our long-interrupted
trips to Fulham where, during my illness, Auntie Kate and
Auntie Jessie had established themselves together in a new
house. Nana and Auntie Noni could join us on visits to the
Zoo. Best of all, my emancipation enabled us to revive the
family custom of spending Sundays on Wimbledon

Common.

After we had alighted from the bus, a leisurely walk across a mile of purple heather brought us to our favourite picnicking place. This was a grove of birch half a mile from the Windmill, the well-known shape of which was visible through the trees. All about us were other little birch-groves, with here and there an oak. To the rear stood a small dark wood where the trees spread their branches above a dense undergrowth of bracken and cool green fern, and where the notes of birds sounded almost eerily in the stillness. Spreading out a groundsheet, we sat or lay in the hot sunshine, the scent of grass and clover in our nostrils and the humming of bees in our ears. Besides roaming in the wood, where snails with beautifully-coloured shells could be picked from the underside of a rotting log, I had of course to keep up acquaintance with my old friends the lizards, catching two or three of them on every visit. Some were bottle green with black markings and yellow-green underparts; some fawn with brown markings and vermilion underparts; and some black with brown and white markings and cream underparts. Father constructed for them a box with sliding glass panels which I called the Lizardry.

Since I fed them several times a day they soon lost all fear of me. In fact I found them very easy to tame. Like most reptiles they liked to have their heads stroked and used to shut their eyes with pleasure whenever I gave them this satisfaction. Toads also had a great fascination for me. My favourite toad, whom I poked out of his hiding-place in the bole of an old tree, where I had seen his eyes shining in the darkness, learned to recognize my voice and would hobble out from behind his log whenever I called him.

Now that I was walking about my parents naturally started thinking it was time for me to return to school.

After an absence of more than two years, therefore, I again went twice daily to the huge brick building down the street. By special permission of the headmistress, I arrived five minutes later than the other children and left five minutes earlier. This was to guard against my being bullied by boys who might have been tempted to take a mean advantage of my defencelessness. Though it was at first assumed that I was far behind the other pupils, I was admitted to the top class of the Junior Department, which most of the boys and girls who had been with me in the bottom class had now reached. Soon after my admission the half-yearly examinations were held. To everybody's astonishment the boy who had not attended school for so long stood twenty-first in a class of about forty. In the next examination I stood sixth and in the one after that came out top of the class, where I remained for the rest of my school career. On account of such precocity I speedily became a favourite with the headmistress, a tall, stout woman whose head was covered with tiny grey curls, and she allowed me to join the small group of children who sat at a table in the hall making rugs.

With my class mistress I was on even friendlier terms. Like her husband in the Senior Department upstairs, she had once taught Father. Though she was older than the headmistress, her hair was a glossy chestnut, and she wore dark blue or brown silk dresses with low V-necks. Whenever she lost her temper, which happened frequently, her face and neck would flush crimson to her very bosom. She it was who gave me such a distaste for Tennyson that it was years before I could enjoy him again. Every child in the class had to learn by heart a verse from 'The Lady of Shalott'. Mine was the one beginning 'She left the web, she left the loom.' Learning poetry by heart I did not mind very much. What hurt me was the way in which we had to chant it in unison, with an exaggerated stress on certain words.

> *She* left *the web*, she left *the loom*,
> *She* made *THREEEE PACES THROUUUUUGH the room.*

This was called giving expression to the poem.

Even worse was the way in which the worthy woman explained each verse.

'*Who* left the room?' she would demand in ringing tones, sweeping the class with a fiery glance.

'Please, ma'am, the Lady of Shalott,' the small voice of one of the brighter pupils would dutifully reply.

'And *what* did she make?' No answer.

'WHAT did she make?' The V-neck was flushing dangerously. After a pause a hand would go up and a timid voice say, 'She made three paces.'

'Yes,' our teacher would boom with grim satisfaction, 'she made three paces THROUGH THE ROOM. And when she had made three paces THROUGH THE ROOM what did she do?'

This question would floor us and the danger-signal would start flashing again.

'She looked out of the window,' ventured someone at last.

'She did NOT look out of the window, you blockhead! Can't you read the poem? SHE LOOKED DOWN TO CAMELOT!!'

Thus the catechism would proceed. In this way we got through the whole poem in the course of about half a term. Probably most of the pupils could not have got through it in any other way; but I have sometimes felt that it might be better not to teach poetry at all than to teach it like this.

But for her sins against 'The Lady of Shalott' Mrs Ainsworth has long had my forgiveness. Like all the other teachers she was, despite her warm temper, a kind-hearted woman who had devoted the best part of forty years to a profession in which the labour is great and rewards few. In my progress and welfare she always took a keen interest. As a mark of special favour I was given the task of making tea for the teachers during the morning and afternoon breaks; for, not being allowed to run about in the playground with the other boys, I had in any case nothing to do. Several of the teachers used to provide out of their own meagre salaries mid-day meals, as well as clothes and shoes, for about a dozen very poor boys and girls, and I had sometimes to keep an eye on boiling peas and potatoes.

When a year had passed in this pleasant fashion I was promoted from the Junior to the Senior Department where, though classes were still mixed, we had masters instead of mistresses, it being no doubt assumed that we now needed a firmer hand.

Like Mrs Ainsworth downstairs and her husband, my new class teacher had taught Father, whom he still remembered. Smoky Joe, as the class affectionately called him, had wavy iron-grey hair and a kind face with lean brown chaps and a humorous mouth. The most striking thing about his appearance, however, was his suits, which could be described only as loud. One was bright ginger, another deep mauve. Changes from one colour to another were of great interest to the class, and when he entered the classroom in a new suit, perhaps even louder than any of its predecessors, we would almost raise a cheer. His method of teaching was, I believe, very good. At least he treated us like intelligent beings who could be induced to understand rather than as morons who could at best be made to memorize. Occasionally he would bark at us, but he never became really angry and never called for the cane and punishment book more than once or twice a term. Though I was with him for only a year he occupies an honoured place in my history, for more than anyone else so far encountered did he encourage my interest in Art and literature. To him I now started bringing the drawings and paintings which I was still industriously producing. Being Art Master for the whole Senior Department he was able to give me not only appreciation, which I never lacked, but hints in matters of technique, wherein I was very weak indeed, He also gave me the freedom of his cupboard, from which I used to borrow a book during breaks, encouraged me in the writing of essays, and gave me my first opportunity of addressing an audience.

At about the same time I developed a love of music. Our music master, a German with a portly figure and fine tenor voice, threw himself with gusto into the task of teaching us the songs of Purcell, Sullivan, and other composers, playing the piano with one hand while conducting with tremendous vigour with the other. My first experience of orchestral music came when all the pupils in the Senior Department were taken to a special children's concert at the Methodist Central Hall at Tooting Broadway. Before the concert began the conductor introduced each instrument in turn to the audience, after which he spoke to us about the compositions we were to hear. The overture *Fingal's Cave* made a deep impression on me, and from that afternoon I had, as it were, an orchestra playing in my brain. Between the orchestral items a stately soprano in an evening gown warbled arias. At the end of every song she descended the dozen or so steps of the rostrum with great dignity and sailed out through a side door. In acknowledgement of our prolonged applause she reappeared, ascended the rostrum, bowed and again descended and disappeared. Since our applause continued, this performance was repeated three or four times. I am sure she had never before had so many calls. But this was not so much because we had enjoyed the arias as because we wanted to see her ascend and descend the rostrum again. By the end of the afternoon the children, not one of whom had attended a concert before, were wildly enthusiastic.

The German music master, who had also played his part in making the concert a success, was very ardently pro-Nazi, and he and Smoky Joe, who was no less strongly anti-Nazi, had many a heated argument in the masters' common room, whence their loud angry voices could be heard down the corridor and even in the hall. This was, for me, the first rumbling of the approaching storm.

Useful though it was at break-time, Smoky Joe's cupboard was not the only source upon which I drew for books. Even before returning to school I had borrowed from the Tooting Public Library, using Father's ticket until I was old enough to join. One of the first books to be carried home was Donnelly's *Atlantis*, which opened for me yet another new world. But being still interested mainly in Art, Archaeology, and History, for some time I confined myself to John Addington Symonds' *The Renaissance in Italy* and Mandell Creighton's *History of the Papacy*, each in six volumes, as well as to the bulky tomes of Mommsen and Maspero. Ancient Egypt and Renaissance Italy indeed cast a spell upon me, and for many months I had no time for any other places or periods.

About the same time that I was thus borrowing books, I started buying them. Ever since my recovery Father had regularly taken me to a curio shop at Clapham Common, not very far from my birthplace, and had sometimes bought curios for the small collection which, with Nana's help, I had begun to build up. On the way we used to pass a secondhand bookshop. Soon boxes and shelves of books, of all sorts and conditions, attracted me more powerfully than suits of armour and old china, and I started visiting the bookshop alone. For me at that time there was no greater adventure than a trip to Clapham Common with a shilling or two in my pocket for secondhand books.

Besides allowing us to spend our Sundays on Wimbledon Common, my emancipation from bed and

51

bathchair made seaside holidays again possible. Our favourite resort was Shoreham, a former fishing village on the south coast, where we always stayed with the white-haired septuagenarian widow of a sea captain. With its heavy green plush tablecloth, and curtains of thick lace, Mrs Bareham's dining-room was almost as old-fashioned as Auntie Kate's. All four walls were covered by photographs of sailing ships, portraits of the deceased sea captain and his son, and huge framed certificates of membership of the Order of Buffaloes, the captain having been many times President of the Shoreham Lodge, as yet another certificate testified. Every inch of space on the piano, the low cupboard, and the side tables, as well as all the little shelves on the many-tiered bamboo mantelpiece, was crowded with china bric-à-brac. Under a glass bell in the corner, standing side by side, were a large stuffed seagull and a child's doll.

On fine mornings we all sallied forth together after breakfast, Joan and I armed with our buckets and spades. Across the toll bridge we went, along the mud-flats where dazzlingly white swans stood cleaning themselves with orange bills, past Bungalow Town with its stony gardens in which sea-thistle and red poppies grew between the pebbles, through the double row of bathing-huts before which old sailors sat chewing tobacco on capsized boats, and down the scrunching pebbly slope that led to the beach. As we approached, the sea-breeze would blow more strongly in our faces, the smell of the ozone grow more unmistakable, the hush-hushing of the sea louder, until at last we saw, perhaps a quarter of a mile below the gently sloping flats of glistening grey sand, the long silvery line of the sea's edge. Afternoons were always spent on the Downs. But the place to which I resorted most often, and with the greatest delight, was the square-towered Norman church, where I spent hours in the churchyard deciphering the barely legible inscriptions on the tombstones.

What my parents thought of my enthusiasm for old churches I do not know, but it had its roots in something deeper than mere archaeological interest. As I stood within their ancient walls, on the spot where, century after century, hearts and voices had been lifted up in prayer and thanksgiving to the Highest, and saw the light slanting red, blue, yellow and green through the stained glass window above the altar, I felt myself breathing an atmosphere of holiness, purity, and peace as tangible as the stones of which the place was built. Whether at Shoreham or Chichester, Norwich or Westminster, thereafter I never missed an opportunity of visiting the shrines of England.

4. 'Here Comes the Boys' Brigade'

A few weeks after we had returned, sunburnt and happy, from one of the Shoreham holidays, we left the old house where I had spent all the eleven years of my life, and moved to a semi-detached council house on the Streatham side of Tooting.

The removal took place in early autumn. What afterwards became father's garden, complete with lawn, flower-beds, and vegetable plot, was then a wilderness. Large yellow-green leaves from the old fig tree behind the house carpeted the ground. Weeds grew shoulder high. Half way down the garden, which was more than a hundred feet long, stood a line of ragged blackcurrant bushes, round which Joan and I were soon playing cowboys and Indians. At the far end, underneath the back fence, was a rhubarb bed. Along the fence on the left grew loganberries which had not been pruned for years. But best of all I remember the chrysanthemums, which grew red and yellow and bronze all over the garden. So many of them there were that all that autumn the air was filled with their acrid scent. Indeed, whether because I had never seen chrysanthemums growing in such profusion before, or because there is a subtle relation between scents and moods, or because they symbolized something I felt but could not express, those frost-bitten blossoms growing so rankly in the neglected garden were one of the major emotional experiences of my life.

One afternoon, not long after our removal, Joan and I heard Mother excitedly calling out to us from the front gate. A strange red glare overspread the whole north-eastern horizon and was reflected above the housetops far up into the sky, where it shaded off into an angry pink. Every now and then a flame would leap up or a wisp of smoke drift black across the crimson. As we watched the glow, which certainly came from no common house-fire, icy fingers of fear for a moment touched our hearts. That evening we learned that the Crystal Palace had been burned to the ground.

The following spring I wrote my first poems. The actual writing of them I do not remember, but I quite clearly recall handing a certain red notebook over the fence to the plump, pigtailed girl next door whom I had told about the poems. With this girl, as well as with her elder sister and younger brother, I had become friends during the winter. My parents had become acquainted with hers. Norah's mother, a Somerset woman, was a paragon of respectability. On Sabbath mornings, sedate in her Sunday best, she could be seen sallying forth to the Methodist Central Hall, which she also attended during the week, being very prominent at prayer meetings and flower shows. Norah and Peter usually accompanied her. At home the children were allowed to play only hymns on the piano. They were frequently scolded, and Joan and I often heard the whack of a cane, followed by a shriek, from the other side of the fence. Norah's father, who was in the police force, fared no better. A hulking, red-faced fellow, he was always being driven out of the house with a broomstick by his plump, pious wife, whose terms of endearment as she thwacked him were clearly audible. After she had withdrawn, slamming the back door shut behind her, he would go and sit beside the chained watchdog, who, also being regularly beaten, would wag its tail in silent sympathy. In this domestic warfare the children took sides, Norah and Peter supporting their mother, and Phyllis, the eldest, their father. Even at that time Phyllis bitterly hated her mother and as she grew older did her best to defend the pusillanimous policeman from the onslaughts of Methodism militant, sometimes carrying the war into the enemy's camp. With all three children Joan and I were on friendly terms and thus it happened that Norah, who was the nearest to me in age, came to be reading my poems that spring.

What I was reading at this time I do not know. Perhaps most of my time was devoted to painting. Certainly it was in the course of the same year that my parents, for the first and last time, discussed the advisability of sending me to an art school. The seventeen-year-old daughter of one of Mother's friends studied at the Slade School of Fine Art and one day she sent me, through Mother, a portfolio of life-drawings. They were all male and female nudes, complete with carefully drawn genitals. Mother and Father seem to have decided that such studies might not be good for my morals, for, though I drew and painted as industriously as ever, there was no more talk of sending me to an art school.

That Christmas I met with a book that swung me, almost violently, from Art to literature. Among the presents at my bedside on Christmas morning was a blue-bound copy of *Paradise Lost*, the title of which had stood high on my latest book list. That morning I had the greatest poetic experience of my life. If it was the reading of Spenser that made a poet of Keats, it was that apocalypse of Miltonic sublimity that made of me, from that day onwards, if not a poet yet at least a modest practitioner of the art of verse. Thereafter I knew no rest until I had planned an epic of my own. What the subject was I do not know, but I remember that it was in blank verse divided stanza-like into blocks of nine lines each and opened with the appearance of a very Miltonic angel in my bedroom. Other poets whom I read, admired, and imitated included Keats, Mrs Browning, and Housman. The first I read in a little pink leather and gilt volume of selections, enjoying most of all the sonnets and the descriptions of Circe from *Endymion* and of the deposed Saturn from *Hyperion*. Mrs Browning's *A Drama of Exile* and *The Lay of the Brown Rosary* I admired inordinately, chanting the latter aloud in my delight to the four walls of my bedroom. Many of the lyrics of *A Shropshire Lad* also made a strong appeal to me, especially the one beginning

'Loveliest of trees, the cherry now

Is hung with bloom along the bough',

which seemed almost the last word in consummate beauty of expression. Rossetti's poems I knew, at that time, only by the quotations in William Sharpe's study of the poet, but meagre as these were the intensely fused sensuousness and mysticism of which they breathed went to my head like some subtle and dangerous perfume. For many years Milton and Rossetti were my favourite poets.

Hard on the heels of my epic, of which I wrote only nine hundred lines, came a mediaeval drama with 'chanters' (borrowed from Thomas Hardy?) and a whole succession of lyrics. Nor was prose neglected. The same period saw the beginning of a 'History of the Reign of Queen Elizabeth', of which I wrote twenty or thirty foolscap pages, a short story about Ancient Egypt in the style of Joan Grant's *Winged Pharaoh*, and 'The Life of Siddhartha Gautama the Buddha' which when finished I copied out in purple ink on my best notepaper.

Meanwhile at school, which I continued to attend, though having a much longer walk every day than before, the curriculum had been disrupted by several events of interest. The first of these had transformed me into a pirate. Included in the Senior Department's Christmas entertainment was a staging of Gilbert and Sullivan's *The Pirates of Penzance*, the rehearsals for which kept us busy for several months. Though I had played Sir Walter Raleigh in an Empire Day playlet while in the Juniors, as well as acted the part of Shylock, in which I had drawn much applause by the way I sharpened my knife on the sole of my foot as I declared 'I will have my pound of flesh', this was the first time I had ever been a pirate. Mother and Father feared the excitement might upset my heart, especially as in one scene the chorus of pirates had to dance a few steps, kicking their legs into the air as they did so. Moreover, on the day of the performance, which was attended by parents, I did not get to bed till one o'clock. However, I was none the worse for the experiment with piracy.

Another disruption was caused by the Golden Jubilee celebrations of the LCC, in which all London schools naturally participated. Our contribution was a topography of south-west London, a subject in which Smoky Joe had done a considerable amount of research. The topography was written page by page on the blackboard from which it was painfully copied by all the children in the class, Smoky Joe having told us that the neatest copy would be sent to the Jubilee exhibition at County Hall. Among other topographical facts I learned that Tooting was named after one Tut, an Anglo-Saxon chief who had sailed up the River Wandle (whence Wandsworth, the name of our borough) and founded a settlement; that Tooting Bec was so called from the Abbey of Bec in Normandy, to which lands there had been gifted shortly after the Conquest; that Nelson had been born at Merton and that Daniel Defoe had worshipped in a Dissenting chapel at Clapham. When, later on, we were taken to the exhibition, I saw my copy of the topography, finely bound, occupying the place of honour in the middle of the hall.

The last of the disruptive events is hardly on the same scale as its predecessors, though it had consequences which to me were not unimportant. For this one Smoky Joe was in a way responsible. While he corrected the exercise books on Friday afternoons it was my task to speak to the class. One day I spoke on 'My Curios', which by that time included a blue silk Chinese robe embroidered with carp and lotuses, a pair of ivory chopsticks complete with knife and silver toothpicks in a silver-mounted ivory case, bamboo nose-ornaments from Borneo, a thunderbolt, pieces of gum-tree (all gifts from Nana), a Chinese monkey with a bag on his back, a little old woman carrying loads, a teak bat carved with peacocks, two halberds from the Tower of London, two Chinese executioner's swords in green leather scabbards, a sixteenth-century Dutch tile depicting Jacob's Ladder, a Moroccan dagger, a Sung Dynasty bowl, precious and semi-precious stones (all from Father), an Indian wire bracelet, a rosary, and sundry foreign coins (from other sources). There was also a small brass incense-burner in the shape of the famous Kamakura Buddha, bought at a Brighton curio shop with my own money, in which I regularly burned sticks of very sweet incense—my first act of Buddhist worship. Smoky Joe asked me to turn the substance of my talk into an essay, and it was this essay which, on its being shown to a visiting inspector, led to my being transferred to a better school.

The institution in which I now found myself was, of course, better than my old school in the opinion of my parents and teachers, in fact of the world generally; but not necessarily in mine. The real source of my education was still the Tooting Public Library. But I donned without protest the uniform of the new school—green cap and blazer with grey flannel trousers—and every day made the slightly longer journey to and from its more exclusive precincts.

On the day of my admission the headmaster sent me to join my class, where a history lesson was in progress. All the double desks were full except two, one of which contained a very blonde girl with roses-and-cream complexion and china-blue eyes, while in the other sat a swarthy girl with black hair and brown eyes. These, as I afterwards found, were the beauties of the class and inseparable friends. Seeing my hesitation, the master called out good-humouredly, 'Take your choice! Which of these two young ladies would you prefer to sit beside?' There was a general titter from the class; the fair one blushed, the dark one smiled.

'If they sit together I can have a desk to myself,' I replied. This arrangement was quite satisfactory to the two beauties who had, before my entrance, been separated for talking during the lesson, and I accordingly took my seat at the desk which the fair one promptly vacated.

Despite the fact of my being two years behind in the course, the headmaster had decided that I should join a class higher than that to which my age entitled me. In the subjects which interested me most, History, English, and Art, I at once went to the top. In Mathematics, which I hated, I stayed somewhere near the bottom. Physics, French, Shorthand, Typing, and Book-keeping were all new to me, but I soon caught up with my classmates. Chemistry, also a new subject, I disliked; but the crusty old Chemistry master, a great rapper on knuckles with the ruler, fortunately was much more a stickler for copperplate handwriting, and neatness of drawing in experiments, then he was for knowledge of Chemistry, and always gave me good marks.

Being still excused games, I spent the games period in the Art Room. The Art master, a small, grey-headed man in sweater and sandals who flirted with the girl students and swore at the boys, was not just an ordinary teacher who 'took Art' but a real artist, the first I ever met. 'Bloody Christ!' he would mutter whenever a student submitted a drawing, 'What do you call this?' With him I soon became well acquainted, sometimes contriving, with his connivance, to be sketching in the Art Room when I should have been doing Geometry elsewhere. He was good enough to correct my drawings, showing me exactly how to make an eye gleam or a petal look soft, things which even Smoky Joe had not taught me.

Even more interesting was a teacher who joined the staff after I had started attending the school, and left before we were evacuated. He was a short, well-built, youngish man with flaming red hair, red moustache, and red beard. Apparently he had only three interests or enthusiasms in life: George Bernard Shaw, atheism, and chess. Thanks to him we read, that is to say listened to, perhaps a dozen of G.B.S's plays. During the History period he read *Caesar and Cleopatra* or *St Joan*, during Geography *The Devil's Disciple*, presumably because its action takes place in the wide open spaces of America, and the rest of Shaw's works during English lessons and on Friday afternoons. In my case this unorthodox method of instruction proved entirely successful. Though I have long since forgotten everything else I learned that year, the memory of these marathon reading sessions, when on hot summer afternoons we had only to sit and listen while he read steadily through the two stout volumes of the Collected Plays, is still fresh and vivid. Atheism was generally inculcated during the morning Scripture lessons which, being nominally a member of the Church of England, he was obliged to take. Chess came in the afternoon, during the last period, and usually continued long after the rest of the school had gone home to tea. Playing twenty or thirty boys simultaneously, moving in a matter of seconds from one board to the next, he invariably defeated us all. Alas! after a few months he was transferred to another school, whether because of the Scripture lessons, or because his appointment had only been a temporary one, we never knew.

With my fellow students I had very little personal contact. Except for my best friend Clement, who was only six months older than I was, all the other boys in the class were senior to me by two years, and the meaningless obscenity of their conversation disgusted me. Besides, shortly after our removal to the new house, I had joined the Boys' Brigade, and for the next four years membership of this organization fully satisfied my gregarious instincts.

At six o'clock one cold November evening, when it had already been dark for more than an hour, Mother and I found ourselves looking, from the opposite side of the road, at the as yet unlit hall in which Brigade meetings were held. Seeing our hesitation, a sixteen-year-old sergeant, in the blue and white Brigade uniform, detached himself from the group of boys talking at the gate and coming over to us asked if he could be of any assistance. Before many weeks had passed I was as keen a member as any in the company. Meetings were held several times a week and I was never absent. On Fridays there were the weekly parades, for which brasses had to be cleaned, leather polished, and piping whitened. After the inspection we were drilled, going through such simple manoeuvres as marching up and down the hall, turning about, halting, and forming fours. All meetings opened and closed with prayer.

The 'officers' who drilled us consisted of the captain of the company, a lieutenant, and two staff officers. The captain, whom the regular members called 'Skipper', was a short, flaxen-haired, brisk little man who worked for a well-known shipping line, on whose behalf he occasionally attended shipping conferences at Rome, Amsterdam, and other places. Besides being our captain, he was superintendent of the Sunday School and held various offices in the Baptist church to which we were attached. The lieutenant, known to us as 'Reg', and the two young staff officers, brothers who had been christened Roland and Oliver, were all teachers in the Sunday school, Reg being, in addition, a sidesman of the church. In due course I started attending not only the parades but also the Sunday morning Bible class, the Wednesday evening prayer meeting, the Thursday evening Morse and semaphore class, and the Monday evening band practice, at which I thumped a side drum.

The company was a small one, never more than sixty strong. Like similar groups the world over, it had a hard core of enthusiasts who could be relied upon to turn up for all meetings with the regularity of clockwork. One of the reasons for which I became one of the band of fifteen or twenty stalwarts whose unflagging devotion it was that, next to the zeal of the captain and officers, kept the company going, was that it satisfied my natural human craving to belong to a group. Another was that the strongly ethical tone of the BB, as we affectionately referred to our organization, with its emphasis on clean living, team spirit, sense of responsibility, service, and fear of God, struck chords in my heart which even poetry and painting were powerless to vibrate. This was all the more the case inasmuch as I saw the qualities of which the BB thought so highly exemplified not only in Skipper and the officers but also, to a lesser degree, in many of the boys. For the latter, therefore, I had a far stronger feeling of brotherhood than for my foul-mouthed associates at school.

But the strongest reason for the almost fanatical punctiliousness with which I discharged the obligations of membership was the one of which I was then least aware.

Among the members was a friendly, affable, good-looking boy about two years senior to me, and for him I at once developed an ardent affection. This early love, to which I remained faithful throughout the whole of my BB career, as well as for some time afterwards, was one of those dumb adolescent attachments which nobody seems to notice, least of all its object. If on raw winter evenings, when more often than not it was raining, or even snowing, I hastened through the dimly lit streets with eagerly beating heart, it was not only because of the thought of the cheery voices that would greet me as I entered the brightly lit hall, but with the hope of seeing, and fear of not seeing, that dearest of all faces. Since Sid was as faithful a member as I was, I rarely had to suffer the pangs of disappointment. But though we met several times a week and were on the best of terms we never became close friends. Strangely enough, this was a deprivation which I never felt. Being utterly happy merely to see his face and hear his voice, it never occurred to me to desire a more intimate relationship.

In accordance with the constitution of the movement, which had been founded as a means of encouraging young men and boys to lead Christian lives, every company of the BB was attached to a church, the priest or minister in charge of which became the honorary 'colonel'. The Baptist church to which our company belonged was a fairly new, red-brick building, complete with steeple, which stood facing Mitcham Lane about half a mile from the top of the road down which I lived. On the opposite corner, also facing Mitcham Lane, stood the Anglican Parish Church. The congregation which filled the red-brick building on Sunday mornings and evenings consisted mainly of prosperous artisans, small shopkeepers, white-collar workers, and other representatives of the petty bourgeoisie from Lower Streatham. During the years in which I was a member of the BB it had as its pastor a man of deep and fervent piety and great preaching ability. Thanks to his ministrations, as well as to the labours of the more devoted of the laity, the congregation grew steadily and the church flourished.

The close connection which existed between the BB and the churches to which the companies were affiliated encouraged, and indeed was intended to encourage, a more active participation on the part of its members in organized religious life. In my case the progression from the church hall, in which Friday evenings parades were held, to the church itself, occurred quite naturally. Our Sunday morning Bible class began at ten o'clock and lasted an hour. We sang hymns of the more virile type such as 'Onward Christian Soldiers', sat with bowed heads through extempore prayers, and listened to a talk of the jocular-muscular variety by Skipper. When these proceedings were over I strolled into church with the other boys as a matter of course, taking my place with them in the gallery, where I sat near Sid.

Below us, at the far end of the church, was a huge pulpit, the size of a small room, from which the pastor not only preached but conducted the service. On either side of this structure were the choir stalls; in front of it was the Lord's Table, whereon always stood a vase of flowers; behind it, the organ. From the back rows of the gallery, where the BB usually sat, only the first two rows of the downstairs pews were visible. Though we sometimes yawned and fidgeted during the long sermon, the BB boys always conducted themselves with proper reverence.

In the gallery I met Mr Young, the elderly stonemason in a very stiff white collar who was sidesman for that part of the church. As he gave each of us in turn a handshake and a hymn book, his deeply lined face lit up with a warm smile. He and Skipper, who was a member of the choir, were both firm believers in the necessity of making a joyful noise before the Lord, and during the singing of the hymns their two voices, raised as in competition, would be heard high above the lusty voices of the rest of the congregation. Mr Young always prolonged the concluding note of each verse much longer than anyone else, frequently ending with a screech that was apt to be rather disconcerting to the newcomer.

He it was, I believe, who invited me to attend the Sunday School, where I joined his class, of which Sid and a few other boys were already members. For some reason or other he took the keenest interest in my spiritual welfare and with great conviction told the rest of the class that the Lord had chosen me out for a great work. Being as he was a Bible Christian of the fundamentalist type, his interest took the form of strong encouragement in the prayerful study of the Word of God. Every quarter he gave me a little book of daily Bible readings of which I regrettably made less use then he had hoped. Occasionally he called on me at home, where he met Father and Mother, who respected him very much for his rugged, almost gnarled and knotted, piety. After my evacuation he sent me the Bible readings by post.

Another member of the church who, though for a shorter period, wrought for me in the Lord, was a plump, almost burly youth of eighteen or nineteen with crinkly hair and a suave, soft manner, called Ben. His attack on the problem of salvation was not quite so frontal as that of my older preceptor. Having started a boys' club, where we played table-tennis on Wednesday evenings, he invited two or three of the more promising members at a time to his house for tea. After a substantial repast, over which his mother presided, we found ourselves, one by one, on our knees in the drawing-room, with Ben, also on his knees, loudly praying beside us. When his prayer, in which he offered up our sinful souls to Jesus, was over, we had to offer them up on our own behalf. In this workmanlike manner he converted a number of boys, for having eaten his excellent tea we felt it would not be good manners to refuse to be saved.

Besides Sunday School and the club, I attended, for a time, the prayer meeting for young men which was held weekly in the vestry. This was the sort of evangelical equivalent of a confirmation class, though here less emphasis was placed on doctrine than on devotion and it was hoped that some, at least, of those who attended would become active church members.

One of the main functions of these meetings was to encourage us in the practice of extempore prayer, to which the Baptists, like most dissenting churches, attached great importance. Kneeling on the ground before our chairs, on the seats of which we rested our elbows, we prayed aloud in turn in such words as we were able to muster. Most of the boys, if not all, borrowed the pious phraseology of their elders, and, with a little practice, were able to offer up prayers with the same unfeeling facility with which they wrote essays at school.

Hymns were sung to the accompaniment of a rather ancient piano-harmonium, which Sid was always glad of an opportunity to play, and there was a Bible reading. Either Reg or Mr Young usually spoke, but once we studied Bunyan's *Holy War* for several weeks in succession with a speaker from another church. On one occasion our own pastor addressed us on the imminence of the Second Coming and Last Judgement, speaking with such eloquent earnestness that I could not help glancing out of the open window at the peaceful, summer evening sky, half expecting to see there angels descending in the van of the Lord.

Yet despite membership of the BB, regular attendance at church and Sunday school, and frequent prayer meetings, the development of my religious convictions was not really influenced at all. This was due partly to the very nature of Baptist Christianity itself, which made not reason but the emotions its chief target, and partly to the fact that I had started thinking for myself in matters of religion. Only once did I have a serious argument. This occurred at one of the vestry prayer meetings, when a boy of my own age maintained that salvation was by faith alone and I declared it was by faith and works. Usually I was satisfied with a temporary emotional exaltation, returning home after a particularly moving sermon with my heart on fire with devotion to the Person of Christ. But at night, when I said my prayers, I still said them, as my habit was at that period, to the Buddha, Christ, and Mohammed in turn, it being my naïve conviction that by this means I should be sure of gaining the ear of whoever happened to be the true saviour.

5. Evacuated

3 September 1939 was a Sunday. As usual we sang hymns and listened to prayers in the Bible class, afterwards filing into church where, after exchanging a few words with Mr Young, we took our customary seats in the gallery. Only one hymn, I think, had been sung when a sidesman ascended the pulpit steps and handed the pastor a slip of paper. Slowly rising to his feet, the pastor announced, not the number of the next hymn, but the fact that our country was at war with Germany. Adding that members of the congregation would no doubt wish to return as quickly as possible to their homes, with a short prayer and a blessing he dismissed us. As we left the church the first air raid warning sounded.

The emotion which filled my heart as I hurried home was neither fear nor sorrow, but exhilaration. Now that the worst had happened the misery of suspense was ended, and it was with something like exultation that I felt my own insignificant life, like a straw on a stream, being gripped by the irresistible current of national events and swept I knew not whither.

For a year Father and the men of his generation had been accustoming themselves to the thought that the war which they had fought to end all wars, to ensure peace to their sons and their sons' sons for ever, had failed. For a second time the lights were going out all over Europe.

At home, at Southfields, and at Ewell, where Father's step-brother Uncle Charles now lived with his wife Auntie Kath, there were anxious family conferences. During the Crisis, in September 1939, the tension had been unbearable, though when Chamberlain stepped with a tired smile from the aeroplane at Hendon waving a piece of paper the general feeling, in our family at least, had been not only one of relief but of defeat. Like many other women, Auntie Kath wrote Mr Chamberlain a letter of thanks and hysterical adulation, receiving in due course a courteous reply. But as the months went by gas masks were issued, Anderson shelters dug in back gardens, and sandbags stacked in front of the doors and windows of public buildings. The BB started a first aid class, Father joined the ARP as a stretcher-bearer, and Joan was evacuated to a farm near Chichester.

During the first few weeks of the war all was in turmoil. But as weeks, then months, slipped by without anything happening, the life of the nation seemed to return from a state of emergency to something very much like normalcy, and the initial feeling of exhilaration began to subside into one of boredom. Gas masks, which we at first religiously took with us wherever we went, buying fancy cases for them to replace the original plain cardboard box, were left at home in cupboards. Father complained that at the ARP headquarters, where he was on duty day and night, there was little to do except play cards in the canteen. As for me, the greater part of the school having been evacuated to safer parts of the country in the previous March and August, I had only skeleton classes to attend twice or thrice a week. Since nothing was taught but algebra and trigonometry I soon ceased to attend them, and with the help of Cardinal Newman and Dr Johnson, Sir Francis Bacon, Heine and the Greek tragic poets, devoted myself more seriously than ever to the task of self-education.

By the summer of 1940 the war had entered its second phase, and it became clear that London would soon know the horrors of aerial bombardment. Fresh arrangements were made for the evacuation of schools and Father insisted that this time I must go.

After a seven-hour journey the train stopped at about three o'clock in the afternoon at Barnstaple, a small town in north Devon. Clement and I, who had resolved to stick together, were taken to the Vicarage, a large house in the best part of the town. From what could be heard of the billeting officers' talk, as they discussed the allocation of evacuees, we gathered that the most difficult part of their work that afternoon would be to find a brace of boys acceptable to Mrs Smith, the Vicar's aunt. Clement and I were selected as the least likely to give her any trouble. In view of what we had overheard it was not without qualms that we followed the billeting officer through the iron gate, up the pathway through the very neglected garden, to the blue and white building that was to be our home.

Before many days had passed we had settled down at the Vicarage and were being treated almost as members of the family which, for such a big house, was a very small one. The Vicar, who in his college days had played rugby, was a very tall, powerfully built man with thinning iron-grey hair and pallid, puffy face which, in contrast to his black suit, showed hardly less white than his clerical collar. Once he had dealt with a truculent beggar by lifting him by the seat of his trousers and the scruff of his neck and throwing him bodily over the front gate. Mrs Smith, his aunt, was a tiny, sharp-tongued woman of seventy-two who was living, so she declared, with only half a lung. Extremely witty and very fond of repartee, she quickly took a liking to me, for, unlike the Vicar, who merely listened with a smile, I could not only take her catches but return them. Poor Clement, a frank, honest, open-hearted youth who blushed easily, she did not particularly like, for though well-mannered he was clumsy in the extreme and whenever she directed her witticisms against him he became embarrassed and confused. To such an extent, indeed, did she succeed in entangling him in his own words that once, when he had something of moment to impart, he first wrote it out and then read it aloud to her in the kitchen like a speech, a procedure which set the mischievous old creature's eyes twinkling in amusement.

Mr Smith, the Vicar's uncle, was a small choleric old gentleman, almost completely bald, who, even with the aid of a stick, moved about with extreme difficulty. He liked to talk about his experiences during the Great War when he had been a special constable in the East End of London. If half the stories he told us were true, it was much more dangerous to walk the streets of Bermondsey after dark then to wander alone in Darkest Africa. At any rate he had sufficient confidence in the ferocity of the female East Enders to declare, with a chuckle, that the best method of executing Hitler would be to let half a dozen of them tear him to pieces with their fingernails—a suggestion of which the prudent Vicar neither approved nor disapproved.

The only other member of the family was the cook, Mrs Levy, a plump, raven-haired Jewess whose husband, an architect, had died in a Nazi concentration camp. She was a cultured woman and talked to me about German literature. Sometimes, not without tears, she spoke of her murdered husband and of the beautiful home from which they had been driven by the Gestapo. Clement, who was very fond of children, used to play with her daughter Sybil, aged five, who soon became very attached to him. But one day Mrs Smith's short temper and sharp tongue proved too much for the overworked refugee woman and after a painful scene she indignantly departed with Sybil in a taxi, taking her luggage with her in seventeen suitcases. The mode of her conveyance and the number of her suitcases scandalized Mrs Smith, who was, apparently, accustomed to servants leaving on foot with small bundles. 'Seventeen suitcases!' she exclaimed, shaking her white head in horrified amazement, 'Whoever heard of a servant having seventeen suitcases!'

Besides being allocated to billets, the evacuees were distributed among the Barnstaple schools, in whose overcrowded classrooms we now pursued our studies. Partly because of its unfamiliarity, partly because my own reading was so far in advance of the curriculum, I developed a hearty dislike for the school which Clement and I attended. The only master (there were no mistresses) I found in the least sympathetic was the Art master. In his classroom, where I also learned bookbinding, I spent my happiest hours. There it was that I produced what was to be my last work of art, an ink drawing of Herod on his throne and Salome kneeling before him with the head of John the Baptist on a trencher. The fact that the nipples on Salome's breasts were clearly delineated gave the Barnstaple boys cause for obscene comment; but the Art master, who had doubtless seen such things before, paid no more and no less attention to them than to the rest of the picture, which he commended highly.

Life at the Vicarage, though certainly neither austere nor puritanical, was naturally rather staid. Amusements were few, though in a moment of abandon Mrs Smith once suggested that we might play croquet with her on the lawn. At five o'clock in the afternoon, when school was finished for the day and we had had tea, Clement and I, now inseparable, used to escape down the road into the countryside. On Sunday mornings we accompanied Mrs Smith to church, where the Vicar conducted the service and preached. Whether due to the modest vestments, or to the murmured plain-chant, or to the fact that the Vicar was by ordination a successor of the Apostles of old, I perceived in the little Anglican church an atmosphere of sacredness which in the Baptist church, for all its cheerful piety, I had never felt.

During our first week at the Vicarage Clement and I had been allowed to listen to news broadcasts, for having relatives in London we were naturally anxious to know whether they were likely to be in danger or not. As the news became daily more ominous, however, we had to leave the dining room a few minutes before these broadcasts began. Mr and Mrs Smith probably wished to spare us the shock of hearing of any sudden reverse. But one day, as soon as the eight o'clock broadcast was over, they called us back to the dining room and with serious faces and solemn voices broke to us, as though it had been the death of a near relative, the news of the fall of France.

Another deadly blow!
Another mighty Empire overthrown!
And We are left, or shall be left, alone;
The last that dare to struggle with the Foe.
'Tis well!

Clement and I had not been able to follow the vicissitudes of the War very closely, for the Smiths had interdicted newspapers as well as broadcasts; but we could understand that what had happened was an unparalleled catastrophe. Even had we failed to understand, Mr Churchill's famous 'blood, toil, tears, and sweat' speech, broadcast a few days later, would have convinced us that our country's plight was even more disastrous than it was in November 1806, during the Napoleonic Wars, when Wordsworth wrote his sonnet—more disastrous than it had been for a thousand years.

Nevertheless, living as I did as much in imagination as reality, I was at that time no less concerned with a war which had been fought three thousand years earlier than the one in which I was personally involved. Clement and I had discovered a stationer's shop which not only stocked new books but displayed outside its door a caseful of second-hand volumes. My first bargain was Chapman's Homer's *Iliad*. Though the poem had long been familiar to me in prose translation, and though I knew all the episodes, it was a new poem that burst upon me that afternoon as I sat out in the brilliantly sunlit garden reading the glorious old fourteeners in the shade of an ash willow. My second bargain was the First Part of Goethe's *Faust*, which produced on me an effect so tremendous, and awoke echoes at a depth so profound, that I was quite unable to analyse its nature and say in what the effect consisted.

We had been exactly one month at the Vicarage and I was beginning to feel at home, when Mrs Smith broke to us, very gently, the news that we were being transferred to another billet. A week before there had occurred an incident which might have had something to do with this unexpected change. One morning, at the time we usually left for school, the rain was streaming down so heavily that Clement and I, who had neither raincoats nor umbrellas, decided that we had better remain at home. When, later in the morning, Mr Smith discovered that we were still in the house he became furiously angry and, with dreadful imprecations for being 'afraid of a little rain', drove us out into the downpour with his stick. On our arrival at school half an hour later, drenched by the storm, we reported the matter to the headmaster, who, seeing how wet we were, sent us back. Whether or not this unpleasant incident was the real cause for our having to leave the Vicarage, all that Mrs Smith told us was that since they now had no servant and had to do all the housework themselves—even the Vicar helping to dry the dishes—and since she had, as we knew, only half a lung, it was impossible for them to look after us any longer.

My first memory of our new billet is of our eating eggs and bacon in the kitchen and the landlady, a thin sharp-featured woman of forty with lank black hair, saying 'It's better than what they gave you at the Vicarage, I'll warrant,' for being a good Wesleyan she had all the chapelgoer's hatred for the Church. Clement, who felt much more at ease than he had done for a long time, wishing to please her heartily agreed, thus winning a grim smile. But I, unwilling to abet in this way any impeachment of the hospitality of our late hosts, remained silent. This did not satisfy Mrs Williams, who repeated her remark, which this time received a non-committal reply.

The four-roomed house in which I now spent my second month as an evacuee was situated in a working-class district on the outskirts of the town. At the end of the little street, behind a heap of slag, lay two or three green fields, the tip of a tongue of countryside that protruded into the urban area. Across these fields Clement and I walked every day to school, which backed on to the green strip. Through the fields meandered a stream. Tall bulrushes and water-flags grew on its banks, where I always lingered to look into the dark waters for the big brown fishes which could sometimes be seen gently moving their fins above the mud.

Since the house was small, with neither front nor back garden, we were allowed to go out more freely than had been the case at the Vicarage. On Saturdays Clement and I used to spend the day at Bideford, a large town twelve miles from Barnstaple. Since I was saving my pocket money to buy books, and since Clement had spent all his buying ice creams for the landlady's two small boys—thus winning more grim smiles and the remark that he, at least, was not mean with his money—we walked the whole distance. On our first visit, which had taken place in our Vicarage days, I had located a second-hand bookshop. Here we spent the whole of every visit, though Clement would doubtless have preferred to see a football match or wander about the town. What delighted me most about it was the number of eighteenth-century calfskin quartos and folios, especially the folio Shakespeare in a dozen or more volumes. Confused and excited by this profusion of riches, I hurried from shelf to shelf, and from room to room, unable to open one book without being immediately attracted by another. When, at five o'clock, it was time to depart, I hastily made my purchases hardly knowing what I was buying.

I also joined the Barnstaple Public Library, which, judging from the number of eighteenth-century editions it contained, must have been originally a private collection. Here I found Johnson's *Works* edited by Arthur Murphy in twelve or thirteen leather-bound volumes, on which I greedily seized. Such was my devotion to my hero that I not only read *The Rambler* and *The Adventurer*, which I admired inordinately, but even his tragedy *Irene*, the verses of which stuck like glue. Since I now devoured collected works and multi-volume editions with ease, I also set to work on Hoole's *Orlando Furioso*, reading a volume a day till it was finished. So omnivorous was my intellectual appetite at this period that one Sunday I read, in addition to the usual instalment of Hoole, Diderot's *Memoirs of a Nun* and all seven of Aeschylus's tragedies. At this time I was utterly devoid of discrimination. Every book I read thrilled and capitvated me and left upon my mind a vivid impression.

One day Mrs Williams took us by bus to the coastal town of Ilfracombe, where she had once lived with her first husband, a seven-foot giant who committed suicide. After wandering the narrow streets that ran up and down the cliff face, I plunged into the nearest second-hand book-shop, emerging a couple of hours later with Boswell's *Life of Johnson*, an illustrated book on Rossetti as a painter, and a leather-bound duodecimo volume dated 1723, in Latin and English, entitled *The Secret Instructions of the Jesuits*. Perhaps it was at Ilfracombe that I also bought *Religio Medici* and *Hydriotaphia*, which I admired so much that I imitated the second of them in an essay entitled 'Of Tombs and Sepultures'. This, apart from an abortive attempt to imitate Hardy, was the sole literary product of my sojourn at Barnstaple, which was about to end.

Kindled by the incident of the eggs and bacon and aggravated by the incident of the ice cream, Mrs Williams's dislike for me had grown bitterer every week. She disliked my preoccupation with books, which she thought unnatural, my manner of speaking, which she jeeringly said was more like that of a man of forty than a boy of fourteen, and my habit of not spending money— except on books, which to her way of thinking was no better than not spending it at all. The thought that though I had ten shillings in my purse I would not spend one penny of it on sweets or ice cream, either for myself or others, infuriated her. One day her dislike flared into open resentment. During tea Reggie, the older of her two young sons, a boy of eleven who naturally took his cue from his mother, spoke to me with such insolent rudeness that, unable to bear the affront, I made him a sharp retort. Mrs Williams's eyes flashed. 'No 'vacuee is going to talk to my son like that,' she declared, after saying exactly what she thought of me. It was not her cold, hard anger that rankled with me so much as the way in which she spat out the term ''vacuee' as though it was the supreme insult. From that day onwards it was open warfare between us. On my side there was either contemptuous silence or a barbed retort; on hers, incessant bitter, jeering abuse. The situation was made worse by her liking for Clement which, in the absence of her young soldier husband, was by that time warmer than it should have been.

Having a thin, weak body, I was ashamed to take off my shirt in front of others. Consequently I always washed in the bathroom. But Clement, who had a good physique, being now nearly sixteen, always stripped to the waist and washed in the kitchen. I often saw Mrs Williams watching him, her hard eyes glittering with lust. Knowing that a few of the older evacuee boys slept with their landladies, whose husbands were also in the Forces, I had no difficulty in interpreting the signs.

Eventually my life in Mrs Williams's house became so unbearable that I asked the street billeting officer, who had accompanied us from London, to find me another billet. She heard me sympathetically but did nothing. I therefore decided to telephone Mother. At the beginning of the war Uncle Charles and his family had been evacuated to Torquay, in South Devon, where his firm was engaged on vitally important war work. Mother had recently gone to stay with him, for the Blitz had started and Father had refused to allow her to remain in London any longer. When I told her that I was unhappy she promised to come to Barnstaple immediately.

What passed between Mother and Mrs Williams, or between Mother and the billeting officer next day, I never knew, but from the look on her face as she emerged from her interviews with them I saw that she had spared neither. On her arrival she had found that the strain of life as an unwanted, indeed hated, "vacuee' had seriously affected my health. Though I had telephoned her only in the hope of getting my billet changed, she decided to take me back with her to Torquay, a decision which I did not question. My only regret at leaving Barnstaple was that two volumes of Johnson's works were still unread.

6. The Veil of Isis

Torquay, as the illustrated brochures of its numerous hotels informed the visitor, was the Riviera of England. Only in Torquay did tropical palms grow in the open air. Only in Torquay could one shut one's eyes against the blinding brilliance of the sunshine and imagine that one was in the south of France, or Italy, or even India. Barnstaple and Bideford were old-fashioned towns of the south-west, towns in which men talked of Drake as though the Armada had been defeated yesterday, and I had not found their atmosphere congenial. But Torquay was different. Barnstaple and Bideford were provincial; Torquay was cosmopolitan. They stood on grey rocks and looked east towards the grey Atlantic; it was built on red rock and gazed south towards

The blue Mediterranean, where he lay,
Lulled by the coil of his crystalline streams.

Perhaps it was no coincidence that my introduction to the Wisdom of the East, my first confrontation with the Veil of Isis, should have occurred at Torquay.

On the day after our arrival Mother had me admitted to the nearest school. This decision of hers I accepted far less quietly than the one which was responsible for my being with her in Torquay at all. In fact, I was still arguing when we reached the school gate. Being now fifteen I wanted to get out into the world, to find a job and work. But Mother's mind was made up, and being wise enough not to argue she countered all my protests with a quiet 'You must finish your education first.'

My last school, which was of the 'open air' variety, was a cheerful, friendly place, and the leniency with which I was excused lessons I did not like soon reconciled me to a further period of Babylonian captivity. Though it had both masters and mistresses, all of whose gowns 'billowed' in true *Gem* and *Magnet* style, my dealings were mainly with the mistresses. Of these, the English mistress, to whose class I was assigned, turned out to be the most sympathetic to my literary aspirations. She was a good teacher, but quite unable to maintain discipline, and the class ragged her unmercifully. So great did the uproar sometimes become that her friend the History mistress, who was as short and fat as the English mistress was tall and thin, would have to come from the classroom next door and restore order. Either because I was well behaved and gave no trouble, or because she divined in me a passion for literature such as she had found in no other boy, the pale harassed woman soon became not only a kindly critic but almost a friend. On my essay on 'The Disestablishment of the Church of England', a subject which gave me the opportunity to air my knowledge of the word 'antidisestablishmentarianism', said to be the longest in the dictionary, and which I had learned from Smoky Joe, she wrote: 'Your command of English is excellent; but you have a tendency to use long words for their own sake. Remember that the best word is the one which most clearly and simply expresses your meaning.' In spite of her sensible advice, it was several years before I could bring myself to sacrifice 'antidisestablishmentarianism' and its 'proud compeers' on the altar of chastity of style.

With her encouragement I began writing, in imitation of Lamb's *Tales from Shakespeare*, a synopsis of *The Spanish*

Tragedy; but the synopsis threatened to become longer than the play itself and I gave up after thirty pages. When I left she gave me a copy of Tennyson's *Complete Poems*, thus breaking down the prejudice set up by Mrs Ainsorth's well-meaning attempts to 'teach' 'The Lady of Shalott', and paving the way for a rich enjoyment of that long-neglected poet.

As there was no room for me in Uncle Charles's house, where Nana was also staying, Mother found me lodgings in a nearby street. Mrs Baker, my landlady, was an elderly woman so short of stature and broad of feature that she looked as though she had been depressed by some gigantic thumb. She spoke very loudly, with an extremely broad Devonshire accent, repeating each phrase two or three times before passing on to the next, as if convinced that every morsel of her conversation was so valuable that the listener should be given as many opportunities as possible to take it in. She was a good cook, but insanely house-proud, and never wearied of directing my attention to the excellence of her possessions. Never, when referring to any object in the house, did she use the definite article: it was always *my* sitting-room, *my* table, *my* dinner, *my* electric light, *my* radio, *my* curtains. Her husband, whom she nagged and scolded incessantly, was a retired light-house keeper. A placid, good-humoured man with a cheery red face, he would wink at me behind his wife's back as she waddled back into her kitchen after a more than usually violent outburst.

Every afternoon I had tea at Uncle Charles's house, which was just round the corner from Mrs Baker's, and on Sundays I went to lunch and stayed for the rest of the day. Though they had given me a very cold reception on the night of my arrival, my aunt and uncle had quickly thawed and once Mother had been forgiven her 'foolishness' in bringing me back with her all was well between us. With

Auntie Kath, who was six or seven years older than Uncle Charles, I had indeed always been on good terms. An intelligent woman with charming manners who had been head librarian at Mudie's, she was extremely thin, with large eyes, rouged cheekbones, and a mass of dark frizzy hair. In Torquay she always dressed in slacks. Mother and Nana used to shake their heads over her housekeeping and it was rumoured she could not cook. Moreover she had an abnormally hearty appetite and consumed huge quantities of food. 'Oh I do love a good tuck in!' she would exclaim as, with shining eyes, she sat down to a meal, frequently attacking it before anyone else was seated. On our visits to Ewell Joan and I had liked her none the less for her peccadilloes, and in Torquay, where she sometimes discussed modern literature and religion with me, I always enjoyed her company. Uncle Charles, who at thirty was already more than half bald, was the chief accountant of a famous British firm. Constant overwork had made him irritable, and there were sometimes rather vicious squabbles between him and Auntie Kath. Though he was as parsimonious as she was extravagant, and moreover inclined to be sadistic, I had always liked him because he was the only uncle young enough to romp and play with me when I was a small boy.

On Sunday afternoons we all went for a walk in the woods near Babbacombe Downs, where we waded ankle-deep in damp dead leaves, picking up dry sticks for the evening fire. Autumn had already come to South Devon. Sometimes, invigorated by the clear crisp air, we followed the precipitous cliff paths far up the coast, pausing wherever there was a gap in the slowly crimsoning forest to look down at the blue-black sea moaning far below. Every now and then fragments of damp white mist would come flying in over the cliff-top. As autumn gave place to winter, the hips and haws showed more and more vividly scarlet among the naked briars.

Before I had been in Torquay many months Uncle Charles was having to spend more and more Sunday afternoons working on his files. Since Mother had returned to London in early autumn, and since Nana did not think it right to leave Uncle Charles alone in the house to make his own tea, Auntie Kath and I sometimes went for our walks alone.

The first thing I did after Mother's departure from Torquay was to leave school and start looking for a job.

Parkes' Coal Company, in whose office in Torquay's main thoroughfare I soon found a situation, was a small concern dealing in coal, coke, and anthracite. Despite the war-time shortage of fuel, business was brisk, for Torquay was a town of hotels, all of which were faced with the problem of keeping their guests warm during the winter. Many a time during the next two months I was to lift the receiver and hear the voice of an irate hotel proprietor demanding to know why the promised twenty tons of whatever it was his furnaces consumed had still not been delivered. One or two proprietors were so utterly unreasonable in their expectations that whenever their voice was heard shrieking from the receiver the whole office groaned. The worst offender, however, was an eccentric baronet who, not long after I had settled in Kalimpong, wrote me incoherent letters on Buddhism without knowing that he had once shouted at me over the telephone for not sending his weekly bag of coke on time. The last arrow in the quiver of an offended customer was always the threat to transfer his or her custom to the rival concern over the road, between which and Parkes' competition was all the more fierce because our senior partner had once been their manager. Their customers must have made the same threat, for during the winter several big hotels were exchanged between us.

Parkes' office was situated above a sweet-shop, with the girl assistants in which I speedily became acquainted, for though not then rationed, chocolate and sweets were often difficult to obtain. The office consisted of the big general office in which the head clerk and the rest of the staff had their stools, the partners' office, a dusty record room where we prepared tea, and a cubby-hole on the next floor where the monthly accounts were made out, two afternoons a week, by an ancient Dickensian clerk in a stiff collar with rheumy eyes and a perpetual dewdrop depending from his nose. When I joined the firm the staff in the general office consisted of Mr Williams the head clerk, a cheerful bald-headed man in spectacles, his assistant, a C3 youth waiting to be called up who swore softly at the partners, the customers, the War, and the world in general as he typed delivery bills on a specially equipped typewriter, and two or three youths a little older than myself who all left before I did. The senior partner was a small, smiling, self-satisfied westcountryman of sixty who was always rubbing his hands together; the junior partner a pink-faced, hefty young Scotsman whose name was identical with that of a well known brand of whisky.

My duties were at first very simple. I answered the telephone, made tea, and delivered bills to the nearer hotels. Not having been able to learn to type by the touch system at school in London, I now adopted the two-finger method, with the help of which I was soon sufficiently proficient to type the numerous letters which the senior partner was in the habit of writing out in longhand just before it was time for me to go home. Office hours were from nine till six, with an hour for lunch, but I usually had to stay till eight o'clock. My wages were ten shillings a week.

Not long after joining Parkes' I signalized my newly-won independence (more apparent than real, for Father still paid all my expenses, allowing me to spend the whole of my wages on books) by moving into more congenial quarters. Now that I had been with her for two or three months Mrs Baker so much regarded me as a member of the family that she included me in all the naggings and scoldings administered to her long-suffering husband. This I did not much mind. But her habit of refusing to allow the electric light to be switched on until at least an hour after dark was a more serious matter. Even though she knew her husband was itching to read the newspaper, and that I was impatient to write down the poems I had composed in the bus coming home, she would sit chuckling in her chair, exclaiming over and over again how pleasant it was to sit in the dark and what a pity that her electricity would have to be switched on so soon. Probably she was not sorry when I left, for ever since the morning that she had found a copy of Swedenborg's *Heaven and Hell* under my pillow she had looked upon me with a feeling akin to horror.

However appropriate the cheerless term 'lodgings' may have been for my room at Mrs Baker's, it was certainly not applicable to the quarters I occupied for the remainder of my stay in Torquay. True I paid—that is, Father paid—a small sum weekly for bed and board, but the kindness and consideration with which I was treated, and the friendliness of every member of the family, made me feel that I had found a second home. Mr French, the head of the family, was a burly inarticulate man of forty of whom, except at weekends, I saw little. His time was divided between the dairy in St Marychurch where I stayed, and the farm from which he supplied the shop with milk, butter, and eggs. In the course of our only serious conversation he solemnly averred that he believed in the literal historical existence of Adam and Eve and seemed astonished that I did not. His wife was a quiet, rather stout woman with greying hair and a toothy smile who had been a teacher. Gwen, Mrs French's unmarried sister, was about thirty-two but looked several years younger. She had light brown hair with a streak of gold in it, grey eyes, a pleasant husky voice and a much gayer and happier temperament than her more serious sister. Mary, the Frenchs' only child, was a fair-haired little girl of five who, for some obscure reason, took a great liking to me almost at first sight. Though by no means fond of children, I could not help liking her in return, and even unbent so far as to allow her to sit on my knee. Being unable to articulate properly owing to some defect, she expressed her feelings towards me by laughing heartily whenever we met. With both Mrs French and Gwen I was soon on a more intimate footing than I had ever been with anyone outside the immediate family circle. For Gwen, indeed, I developed a very deep attachment. What was stranger, she became extremely fond of me.

My late hours at Parkes' Coal Company during the week, and my walks with Auntie Kath on Sunday afternoons, left me with much less time for reading than I had enjoyed either in London or at Barnstaple. Yet I continued to read in a week more than the average boy of my age read in a year. Some of the books I consumed at this time exercised a decisive influence on my whole life and thought. Among my discoveries was Schopenhauer, in whom I at once recognized a kindred spirit. Classical authors included Plato (in the complete Böhn translation), Aristotle, Theocritus, Longinus, Demetrius, Tyrtaeus, and Lucian, but my most ardent admiration was for Seneca and the Emperor Julian. The ethical sublimity of the Roman moralist struck for the first time a chord which has vibrated in me ever since. Strange to relate, it was not from the Bible or *The Holy War*, but from the *De Beneficia* and *De Consolatione*, that I learned not only to love the good life but to strive after it. Why I admired the writings of the Emperor Julian is not clear to me. Perhaps it was the 'archetypal' semi-orientalism of his religion that appealed to me, for I was becoming more and more attracted to the exotic in literature.

Neither the Torquay nor the Barnstaple Public Library had a section devoted to the literatures of the East. But at Torquay, after the Russian and other minor European literatures, half a dozen volumes did their best to represent the vast riches of Chinese, Japanese, Sanskrit, Persian, and Arabic prose and poetry, philosophy and religion. As soon as I saw these books there flashed upon me, like a revelation, the thought, 'Why should I limit myself to Europe?'

Of the Torquay Public Library's oriental section, the whole of which I probably read, I now remember only *The Yoga of the Bhagavad Gita by Shri Krishna Prem, an English Vaishnavite with whom I subsequently corresponded, Noh Plays of Japan*, and the *Dabistan*. But from that day there grew upon me the conviction, afterwards immovably implanted in the centre of my consciousness, that regionalism or nationalism in literature or art, philosophy or religion, is an anachronism. Why should not the cultured Englishman be as familiar with Li Po in translation as he is with Shakespeare in the original, or the German philosopher as well acquainted with the doctrines of Nagarjuna as he is with those of Kant? Why should not the West be as receptive to Eastern culture in the twentieth century as she was to Graeco-Roman art and literature in the fifteenth? Whether he is born in Europe, Asia, Africa, America, or Australasia, and whether he be a Buddhist, Christian, Muslim, Hindu, Zoroastrian, Jew, Confucian, Taoist, Shintoist, Animist, or atheist, the true citizen of the world should aim at a broad acquaintance with all that is best in the whole cultural and spiritual heritage of mankind.

Having exhausted the Torquay Public Library's stock of

oriental literature, I turned to the stationers and book-sellers opposite Parkes'. Here I found, in the Everyman series, *Hindu Scriptures* and Kalidasa's *Shakuntala*. In the first, a volume of selections from Hindu religious litera-ture, I particularly admired the Vedic hymns, especially those addressed to Ushas, the Dawn; the Upanishads I found obscure. Compared with the plays of Marlowe and Ben Jonson, all of which I had read while still with Mrs Baker, *Shakuntala* seemed rather poor stuff—even after making all possible allowance for the difference, really not very great, of dramatic convention. In India Kalidasa is always compared with Shakespeare; but when, willing to revise my early judgement, I read *Shakuntala* again seven-teen years later, I was obliged to ratify it instead. However, the lovely imagery of the *Meghaduta* or 'Cloud-Messenger', a long lyric poem, delighted me immensely. Shortly after-wards, in the same bookshop, I found *The Song Celestial*, Sir Edwin Arnold's famous verse translation of the *Bhagavad Gita*. This gave me even greater satisfaction. In-deed, I used to read the eleventh book, 'The Vision of the Universal Form,' in a state bordering on ecstasy.

> *Then, O king, the God, so saying,*
> *Stood to Pritha's son displaying*
> *All the splendour, wonder, dread*
> *Of His vast Almighty-head.*
> *Out of countless eyes beholding,*
> *Out of countless mouths commanding,*
> *Countless mystic forms enfolding*
> *In one Form, supremely standing*
> *Countless radiant glories wearing,*
> *Countless heavenly weapons bearing,*
> *Crowned with garlands of star clusters,*
> *Robed in garb of woven lustres,*
> *Breathing from His perfect Presence*
> *Breaths of every subtle essence*

> *Of all heavenly odours; shedding*
> *Blinding brilliance; overspreading—*
> *Boundless, beautiful—all spaces*
> *With His all-regarding faces;*
> *So He showed! If there should rise*
> *Suddenly within the skies*
> *Sunburst of a thousand suns*
> *Flooding earth with beams undeemed-of,*
> *Then might be that Holy One's*
> *Majesty and radiance dreamed of!*

Whether I appreciated such lines more as poetry or religion would be difficult to say. Sometimes it happened that when I thought I enjoyed a poem, I really responded to a religious teaching, and when I thought I responded to a religious teaching I in fact enjoyed a poem. But of my reaction to the work that now brought me face to face with the Veil of Isis there could be no uncertainty.

One Saturday afternoon, as I was changing books, I noticed on a door in the Reference Room the words 'Moyse Collection'. On my application to the librarian the door was unlocked and I found myself in the midst of the biggest and richest collection of books I had yet seen. Resisting the very strong temptation to describe in detail the excursions into the Greek and Latin classics, Old English texts, and Elizabethan drama which I thenceforward made on Saturday afternoons (for the books belonging to this collection had to be read on the spot), I shall confine myself to two volumes which were my stepping-stones to higher things. The first of these was Hartmann's *Paracelsus*. Though the work interested me deeply, I was still more interested by its constant references, usually in footnotes, to *Esoteric Buddhism*, a work of which I had never heard. Coming upon it one afternoon not far from *Paracelsus*, I promptly read it. Much more vividly than the vague sense of widening horizons which it gave me do I remember its constant references, also in footnotes, to another work of which I had never heard: *Isis Unveiled*. This was not available in the Moyse Collection, but I discovered it soon afterwards in the Lending Department and bore the two bulky volumes back with me to St Marychurch.

How shall I describe their effect upon me? Though in itself almost entirely negative, it proved to be more far-reaching in its consequences than that of any book I had previously encountered. Within a fortnight I had read both volumes twice from cover to cover. Impressed, be-wildered, thrilled, excited, stimulated as I was by their staggeringly immense wealth—their 'inexhaustible truck-loads,' as Maeterlinck called them—of information on every conceivable aspect of philosophy, comparative religion, occultism, mysticism, science, and a hundred other subjects, the realization which dawned most clearly upon me, and which by the time I had finished stood out with blinding obviousness in the very forefront of my consciousness, was the fact that *I was not a Christian*—that I never had been, and never would be—and that the whole structure of Christian doctrine was from beginning to end thoroughly repugnant to me. This realization gave me a sense of relief, of liberation as from some oppressive bur-den, which was so great that I wanted to dance and sing for joy. What I was, what I believed, I knew not, but what I was not and what I did not believe, that I knew with utter certainty, and this knowledge, merely negative though it was as yet, gave me a foretaste of that freedom which comes when all obstacles are removed, all barriers broken down, all limitations transcended.

The effects of this great emancipation were for the time being insignificant. In an attempt to give it a positive content I plunged into Swedenborg's *Arcana Celestae*, into the study of Hebrew, into the *Key to Theosophy*, into

Rosicrucianism; but not until a year later, in London, did I find that for which I was searching. *Isis Unveiled* could not help me. Indeed, the title originally chosen by the author had been 'The Veil of Isis'; but the publishers, alive to the publicity value of the suggestion of secrets revealed, changed this to the title under which it subsequently became famous. It is a curious fact that though I at first assumed that the author, H.P. Blavatsky, was a man, by the time I had finished it I knew, intuitively, that *Isis Unveiled* had been written by a woman. Though it was an incomparably greater Hand that lifted for me the Veil of Isis, she has my undying gratitude for having brought me where I could see it face to face.

At Parkes' Coal Company my position had been steadily improving. As one by one they left I took over the work, first of the two or three youths, then of the C3 swearer, and finally of Mr Williams. The last in the coal office had become the first. Instead of handing over calls to more experienced members of the staff, I now took orders, soothed irate hotel proprietors, and explained the current coal situation. When customers called at the office, I accepted payments, issued receipts, and assured them that their next consignment would be delivered without delay. (Among the callers was Agatha Christie, who was on our books under her real name.) Twice or thrice a week I went to our petrol dump, the keys of which were now in my keeping, watched while the drivers filled the tanks of their lorries, and took dippings of the amount remaining with a notched steel yard. On Friday afternoons I paid the foreman, drivers, and delivery men their wages at the coalyard adjoining Torquay Station.

My biggest job, however, was the daily typing of delivery bills on the specially equipped typewriter, the intricacies of which I had now mastered. On busy days this kept me hard at work from two in the afternoon until six in the evening. After being typed the delivery bills had to be checked by the senior partner. As we were supposed to close at six, and as this part of the work sometimes took two hours, the checking should have started at four. But in the days when the C3 youth officiated at the typewriter, it was the senior partner's pleasant habit to waste the whole afternoon gossiping and then, at six o'clock, to sit down with a gay smile to do the checking. My indispensability now enabled me to put a stop to this imposition. At four o'clock I would look at the clock above the mantelpiece and remark that I wanted to leave 'early' that evening. This was office parlance for 'not later than six-thirty'. After I had done this three or four times the hint was taken and the checking of orders sometimes started as early as three o'clock.

Our shortage of staff reduced the junior partner, who having put more money into the business had more prestige to maintain, to the practice of some strange subterfuges. One of these I witnessed several times before understanding its significance. Whenever, owing to my preoccupation at the typewriter, he had answered the telephone himself, he would gently lay down the receiver, quietly rise to his feet, and having stolen tiptoe across the room to the far corner would stand there for a minute as if lost in thought. Then springing suddenly to life, he would stride rapidly to the telephone, crashing his heels into the floor as he did so, and picking up the receiver shout 'Hullo, hullo! Yes, speaking!' in loud cheery tones.

Though I worked very hard during my last two or three months in the coal office I was quite happy there, and while not actually liking the work, took an interest in it and did it to the best of my ability. My wages had more than doubled, for after the departure of the C3 youth I asked for a rise, and after the departure of Mr Williams the partners gave me another of their own accord. Higher wages to me, of course, meant more books. After the hints about wanting to go 'early' I was often able to leave the office at six, instead of at eight as before, which left me more time in which to enjoy the pleasant company of Mrs French and Gwen. It also gave me time for the study of the Rosicrucian literature which I now received every fortnight from San José, California.

The advertisements of the Ancient and Mystical Order Rosae Crucis (AMORC) are well known to the readers of the occult, spiritualist, or universalist type of periodical. They even appear in newspapers and magazines. How my eye was first caught by one of them I do not recollect; but evidently the prospect of being initiated into the ancient mysteries appealed to me, for I was soon spending a substantial portion of my wages on the various dues. Of the rather nebulous contents of the green folders which came every two weeks in plain covers, thus greatly intriguing Mrs French and Gwen, both of whom wondered who the mysterious correspondent in the United States could be, only vaguely beautiful impressions now remain. The memory of a certain 'initiation' remains vivid, however, because it was the occasion of my hurting, quite unintentionally, the feelings of my two friends.

This 'initiation' consisted, as far as I can remember, in lighting a number of candles in front of a mirror and then gazing with concentration into the mirror until the Rosy Cross appeared. Now since there was no electric bulb in my room, I was supplied with candles, by the light of which I used to read at night. Not wanting to ask for an extra supply, for the ceremony had to be kept secret, I bought a packet on the way home from the office. At lunch the next day the sisters gently reproached me for buying candles myself instead of asking for them, for while cleaning my room they had noticed the remains of the packet I had purchased in a half-open drawer.

As spring gave way to summer, Auntie Kath, Uncle Charles, Nana, and I began spending either the mornings or the afternoons on Sundays down on Babbacombe beach. Never, in England, did I enjoy such perfect weather in such perfect surroundings. Behind us the red sandstone cliffs rose sheer for three or four hundred feet. Before us lay the shimmering, intensely blue width of the sea, from which the sun struck little sparkles of gold. Between the two stretched a ribbon of dazzlingly white beach, and overhead, from horizon to horizon, the quivering blueness of the sky.

But when Father, who throughout the Blitz had worked day and night as a stretcher-bearer, came to Torquay for a short holiday, I started feeling homesick. After giving notice to the partners, who spent my last days gloomily reconciling themselves to the prospect of having a girl in the office, and bidding an affectionate farewell to Mrs French and Gwen, I returned to London after an absence of one year.

7. The Pendulum Swings

The two-and-a-half years which followed my return from Torquay were among the most important of my present existence. Every aspect of my being, from the lowest to the highest, sought eagerly for the fullest possible unfoldment and expression, so that my life was during this whole period a chaos of conflicting impulses. My love of art, of literature, of music, already sufficiently ardent, became a ruthless passion. Books, never chewed or merely tasted, were now indiscriminately swallowed whole in a fruitless attempt to satisfy an appetite frightful in its ravenousness. My senses, practically dormant until then, suddenly awoke and clamoured for satisfaction. For the first time in my life came psychical and mystical experiences. Though heights were touched, existence for me consisted not in progress but in a perpetual violent oscillation between extremes. Small wonder that the heroes of this period were stricken, tormented, demoniacal figures—Strindberg, Nietzsche, Beethoven.

The London of 1941 was not the London of 1940, any more than the youth who returned from Torquay was the boy who had been evacuated to Barnstaple. The Blitz lay between. In nearly every street great gaps showed in the rows of houses as noticeably as missing teeth in a human face. The populace, though in the mass cheerful, confident, and determined, now that frightfulness had done its worst, and failed, was in individuals beginning to exhibit signs of strain.

How great a test of endurance the Blitz had been was clear from Father's tales of the period when, night after night, he and the rest of his squad had rescued the trapped and the injured, and removed dead bodies from the wreckage of bomb-shelters, sometimes from blazing buildings, while bombs were still falling in other parts of the city and while the earth rocked and quivered beneath them and the anti-aircraft guns pounded away as, in the blackness of the sky, the searchlights darted hither and thither trying to pick out the tiny dark shapes of the bombers. His worst experience, however, had been not during but after an air raid, when his squad helped remove the bodies of the three thousand people, mostly women and children, who were drowned the night a water main, struck by a bomb, had burst and flooded the tube shelter in which they had taken refuge.

Yet even the Blitz had not been without its comic aspect. Once, during a particularly heavy bombardment, when the singing of shrapnel filled the air, Father left the house in such haste that he forgot to put on his steel helmet. Noticing it on its peg in the hall a minute later, Mother seized it in her hand and heedless of the shrapnel ran bareheaded up the street crying, 'Phil, Phil, you've forgotten your helmet!'

At the time of my return to London the Blitz had not quite petered out, and from the few air raids I experienced I was able to imagine what it must have been like at the height of its fury. Not that I had never heard bombs falling before. At Torquay, one night, six or seven had been dropped in a line, the first a hundred yards from the house, the last in an open field five miles away. Each time the whistle had seemed shriller and the crash more deafening than before; but instead of falling nearer, as I thought, the bombs were in fact falling further away and the last, being the biggest and loudest, seemed the nearest. Indeed, it seemed to explode directly over my head. The following morning Gwen and I went to see the damage done by the nearest (and smallest) bomb, which had destroyed two houses and injured several people. ,

In London, of course, the whistle and crash of bombs was only part of the proceedings. Much worse were the ear-splitting detonations, four or five at a time in quick succession, of the nearby ack-ack guns, especially of the mobile unit which sometimes operated from the top of the road. Much practice had made the gunners expert, and many a time did Father and I, standing out in the garden, see the enemy planes falling in flames to the ground. With so much artillery fire the danger from flying shrapnel was no less than that from falling bombs, but long experience of the Blitz had intensified the strain of Anglo-Saxon fatalism in the English character, and though few took unnecessary risks the general attitude was, 'If your number's on it, you'll get it; if it isn't, you won't.' Within a few weeks I had become as phlegmatic as other Londoners. At breakfast on mornings after particularly noisy raids Father used to relate how, thinking I must have been disturbed, he had looked into my room during the night and found me fast asleep.

The worst experience which awaited me on my return to London had nothing to do with the Blitz. One day, while reading the newspaper, I became aware that my parents were talking to each other as I had never heard them talk before. Like all husbands and wives they had quarrelled occasionally, but never had such bitter words been exchanged between them. Horrified, I listened from behind the newspaper.

'Yes, and you brought your son back from Torquay to spy on me!' exclaimed Mother in a fury.

'Son, tell your mother whether I brought you back or whether you came of your own accord,' said Father in an injured, sorrowful voice. Without lowering the newspaper, I burst into tears. Father waited until my sobs had subsided, then took away the newspaper and gently repeated the question. He looked worried and miserable. Mother's averted face was hard and cold.

'I came of my own accord,' I said amidst sobs.

Much as this incident lacerated my feelings at the time, I soon ceased to think about it. The storm having perhaps cleared the air, relations between Father and Mother were again harmonious and I was busy reviving old connections and forming new ones.

Having exhausted such resources of the Tooting Public Library as appealed to me, I began to rely more and more on its counterpart at Streatham. In addition to Gnosticism, Rosicrucianism, and Neoplatonism, I took up the study of Chinese history and culture, began reading biographies of the great composers, started teaching myself Arabic and New Testament Greek, and opened up a campaign against Philosophy by storming two of its strongest citadels: Kant's *Critique of Pure Reason*, which I read thrice, and Hegel's *Philosophy of Religion*.

Attempts to revive my old connections with the BB were less successful. Where our hall had once stood was a large empty space and several piles of rubble. For two weeks I attended parades and Bible classes in the hall of the Anglican church across the road, whose company and ours were now amalgamated; but most of the old familiar faces were gone and the atmosphere was different. Besides, having realized in Torquay that I had never believed in Christianity, the hymns and prayers now seemed empty and unreal. Perhaps Skipper sensed the change in me. Or perhaps I was anxious to share my new understanding. Whichever it may have been, I have a vague recollection of trying to convince him of the necessity of an impartial study of all religions and of our both feeling, at the end of the discussion, that we now stood very far apart.

As air raid warnings became rarer, Mother and I started going out together, making trips to the National Gallery, where a single masterpiece was on exhibition at a time, and to Westminster Abbey. Once we went to Westminster Cathedral with Auntie Kate, who lit candles and said prayers while Mother and I watched the priests officiating at the high altar, and once we went to see Mother's eldest brother, whom I had never met. But even more than churches and museums, which were my passion rather than hers, Mother loved shops and restaurants. Her most serious complaint against Father had always been that from one year's end to the next he never took her out for an evening's entertainment. Though by nature sociable, he preferred his own fireside, or a quiet hour at the public house with friends, to the artificial glitter and hollow gaiety of the fashionable West End restaurants, or the tawdry pseudo-Gothic splendours of the local cinema.

Having no children of school age, and being under forty-five, Mother had been required to register for part-time national service. Either shortly before or shortly after my return from Torquay she and her friend Margaret joined the Education Department of the LCC. The branch in which they worked, then conveniently located in the deserted buildings of a nearby kindergarten, was responsible for the supply of equipment to evacuated schools. So much did Mother like this work, and so capable an administrator did she prove, that within a few months she was transferred from the part-time to the full-time staff and promoted to assistant head of the branch. This meant that she no longer had time to cook lunch, so at twelve o'clock each day she and I and Margaret went to a restaurant at Tooting Broadway. With us came Mother's chief, the head of the branch, a small, unobtrusive, kindly man of about fifty-five.

With Father on duty at the ARP headquarters, in the evenings Mother and I were generally alone. As she sat silently mending socks and shirts hour after hour there would sometimes escape from her a sigh of sheer weariness which, though it pierced me to the heart, I ignored and went on reading. If she ventured a remark I answered with a grunt. After leaving England I bitterly regretted this selfish behaviour, the memory of which filled me with grief and shame. Never in my life was the aesthetic so inimical to the ethical. If she wanted to listen to the Forces Programme I curtly told her that it would disturb me; but if I wished to listen to Bach or Beethoven, which gave her a headache, I switched on the radio without caring for her feelings. Later on, Joan and I always quarrelled about the radio, which I took into the sitting-room, where there was an extra plug-in, whenever I wanted to listen to the Promenade Concerts. Since Joan was good-natured and I bad-tempered she usually gave in to me, but if one of her favourite crooners was on the air she insisted on her rights. On such occasions I did sometimes give in, though with a very bad grace; but if a symphony or concerto which I particularly wanted to hear was being broadcast over another wavelength I would go to any lengths of rudeness and ill-temper to get my own way. With Mother there was never any dispute. Besides being accustomed to me having my own way, she was naturally of a gentle, patient disposition. Once, in a moment of exasperation, she exclaimed, 'You're just like your father—obstinate as a mule!' But such outbursts were rare. Thus it was that she submitted to evenings of sheer boredom without a word of complaint, darning socks and turning the wrists and collars of shirts with war-time economy, while I read philosophy and religion or listened to classical music on the radio.

Though I had responded to classical music ever since that afternoon I had heard *Fingal's Cave* at the Methodist Central Hall, only after my return from Torquay did it become an addiction. Bach's *Toccata and Fugue in D Minor*, which seemingly explores the heights and depths of the universe, occupied in my experience of music a place analogous to that of *Paradise Lost* in my experience of poetry. Stunned, overwhelmed, annihilated by those majestic chords, I went about for several days in a kind of waking trance. As soon as I came to my senses I tried to translate my experience of the music into poetry. Later on, in fact, I wrote in imitation of Baudelaire's 'Les Phares' a poem on all the great composers from Bach to Delius, as well as a dramatic idyll on Beethoven.

My enjoyment of music was far more intense than that of poetry had ever been. This was partly due to the very nature of music, which unlike poetry is pure feeling devoid of all cognitive content, and partly to the fact that at this period I craved for constant emotional intoxication. My two favourite composers, that is to say those by whom I was most strongly stimulated, were Beethoven and Tchaikovsky. When the violence of my feelings had subsided I preferred Mozart and Haydn, while Bach remained a constant favourite.

Whether the intensity of my enjoyment of music contributed to my first mystical experience, which came at about this time, I am unable to say. But a Beethoven overture or a symphony by Mozart used to affect me so powerfully that for several days I would hear the music ringing again and again in my ears. So intense, indeed, would my concentration on these inner sounds be, that not only did they sound as loud and clear as when I had heard them with my physical ears over the radio, but I would practically lose consciousness of my body. This state of semi-trance which music sometimes induced in me seemed to be of the same order as the two experiences which, appropriating a conveniently vague term, I have called mystical.

Both occurred several times. The first had indeed come to me, though not very intensely, even before my evacuation. Like most of my other mystical experiences, it is associated in memory with the place at which it occurred. One day, on my way to the Tooting Public Library, I as usual had to cross the road at Amen Corner—so called because in ancient times, when the choir of the parish church performed the annual ceremony of 'beating the bounds,' they broke up at this spot, which marked the boundary of the parish, with a loud 'Amen'. As I crossed from one side of the street to the other I suddenly awoke to the complete absurdity of the mind being tied down to a single physical body. Why could I not look at the world through the eyes of the man standing on the opposite pavement? Why could I not know his thoughts as easily as I knew my own? As these questions flashed upon me I felt my consciousness desperately struggling to free itself from the body and project itself into all the bodies walking round Amen Corner. Though its efforts were unavailing and it sank back exhausted I thereafter had a feeling of being imprisoned. When years later I read in the *Surangama Sutra*, a famous text of Buddhist idealism, the dialogue in which the Buddha makes his disciple Ananda realize, step by step, that his consciousness is neither inside the body nor outside it, nor yet somewhere between, being in its true nature universal, I felt I was treading on familiar ground.

The other experience was even more striking. As I was walking down the main road towards Tooting Broadway, it suddenly seemed as though I was moving in a world of ghosts. The whole street with its houses, shops, and people suddenly receded into the infinitely remote distance. The roar of the traffic faded into an intense silence. My own body felt light, airy, insubstantial, and it seemed I no longer walked on the solid pavement but floated, clearly conscious, through an immense void. This void was simultaneously conterminous with my own consciousness, so that it also seemed that I was floating through myself. Though this experience, which was much more vivid than the first, generally lasted for the time it took me to walk a hundred yards, its after-effects persisted much longer; for upwards of an hour the objective world, though again visible, seemed strangely unreal, as if it had no business to be there and might disappear any second. My subsequent study of Buddhist literature confirmed this experience too. When I read in the *Lankavatara Sutra* and other works that one must meditate on the world as being in reality like a dream, I at once understood what was meant.

After two or three months at home I began to feel that I should work again. This time Mother raised no objection. At the suggestion of Sid, Mother's chief, I applied for a clerical post in the Public Health Department of the LCC and after a rather perfunctory interview entered the service of the biggest municipality in the world.

8. Buddhism and the LCC

How many storeys County Hall Main Block consists of I do not remember, but they contain six hundred rooms and twelve miles of corridor. North Block and South Block, between which one passes on the way to the Main Block, though each containing the same number of storeys cover a much smaller acreage. The Public Health Department occupied the whole of the fourth floor. The branch to which I was allocated, and in which I worked for two years and four months, was tucked away in the north-east corner next to the office of the Medical Officer of Health, who was the head of the whole department. It consisted of four rooms: a small one overlooking an inner courtyard for the Chief, his deputy, and his personal assistant (myself), a large room for the woman and girl clerical assistants, the number of whom varied from six to eight, a room for the three matrons, and a waiting room.

The Chief was a short, cheerful, easy-going man in his early forties. Unlike most of the other members of his grade he was of working class origin and instead of joining straight from university had worked his way up from the lower ranks. His deputy was a dull, colourless man in his late thirties with a pale unhealthy complexion and astonishingly bass voice. Of the women and girls in the general office all except two either left after I joined or joined before I left.

The two exceptions were Thelma and Miss Cook. Thelma, who remained twenty-nine for the whole time I knew her, though she celebrated several birthdays, was a bold-eyed, black-haired wench who darkened her naturally swarthy complexion by the liberal application of reddish-brown pigment. In my memories of her she invariably wears a cabbage green costume, though I suppose she must occasionally have worn something else. Originally a punching machine operator, she still belonged to the technical grade, but through intrigue had managed to get herself transferred to a post in the higher clerical grade. Between her and the long-suffering Miss Cook there was a deadly feud.

Miss Cook, the cousin of a famous counsel, was the seniormost member of the general office, having joined the service before most of the girls were born. Of slightly 'Jewish' physiognomy, she liked to relate how her friends called her an old Jewish matriarch. Short-sighted, with her grey hair tumbling about her face, she peered at papers over the tops of her spectacles. Always much better dressed than any of the girls, she sometimes appeared on Saturdays in voluminous black taffeta that rustled loudly as she moved.

Between Miss Cook and me relations were cordial. Once, when I had been rather impudent, she banged me over the head with a file; but this act of exasperation only cemented our friendship. During the Chief's lunch hour she would sit on the edge of my desk and talk to me. Her favourite topics were the Kabbala, the poetry of Swinburne, and her experiences as a worker in the Social Welfare Department. Though I was sixteen and she sixty-five, this rather Victorian old lady never hesitated to describe the seamiest aspects of life in the East End, with which, indeed, she had a very extensive acquaintance. Due to the matter-of-fact way in which she spoke of rape, incest, prostitution, and venereal disease, I was able from that time to discuss these subjects without embarrassment.

Miss Gretton, the Head Matron, could hardly have been less than fifty-five and might well have been considerably more. Her hair, which sometimes showed white at the roots, was a kind of carroty-brown, and round it she wore a green velvet fillet. Her face was a mask of powder, rouge, lipstick, and mascara, all heavily applied. On her fingers, the long nails of which gleamed bright scarlet, she wore numerous rings, the most noticeable being mounted with a thick silver plate, about two inches square, engraved with what she claimed were Hebrew characters. Her dresses, which she wore very short, were full of the most vivid reds, greens, and violets. In the office she never put her arms into the sleeves of her coat, but sat with it draped around her like a cloak. At her throat were several strings of artificial pearls. When she stood, she looked so round-shouldered as to be almost a hunchback. Nothing was known of her origins, but on the strength of the fact that her private nursing home had been bought by a member of the royal family she apparently considered that she belonged to the aristocracy. To women of the working class who came for interviews she could be unspeakably rude. Middle-class women were treated with haughty condescension. To titled women she was all graciousness.

The two other matrons, who had been in charge of big London hospitals, were between sixty-five and seventy. Both were white-haired and plainly dressed, and neither wore make-up. Though of rather severe demeanour they were quiet, ladylike, and courteous.

The Civil Nursing Reserve, as the branch was called, had been formed by the Ministry of Health as a means of supplementing the nursing staff of hospitals in London and the Home Counties, where air raid casualties had imposed a severe strain upon the resources of all such institutions. Its work consisted in the recruitment, training, and allocation of personnel. These simple functions were not, however, discharged without considerable friction between the various agencies involved, as well as between members of the staff of each agency. In the CNR the friction was mainly between the Chief and Miss Gretton. This was only a reflection of the antagonism which ran through the whole department.

Unlike certain other departments, Public Health was divided into a hierarchy of four grades as rigidly defined and (with the exception of the MOH, a professional man with administrative functions) as mutually exclusive as the four castes of Hindu society: technical, clerical, administrative, and professional. Between the matrons, who belonged to the professional grade, and the heads of branches, who belonged to the administrative grade, went on a continual cold war. The matrons, while jealously guarding their supreme authority on all 'professional' matters, were constantly trying to usurp functions which were strictly administrative, an encroachment which the administrative staff vigorously contested. These skirmishes usually resulted in victory for the administrative side, by whom the line of demarcation between the two spheres of jurisdiction was better understood and more scrupulously respected.

After the question under dispute had been carried up to the MOH for decision, a defeated matron would airily remark, 'I thought it was a professional matter,' or, if the encroachment had been particularly flagrant, 'I don't know what difference it makes if I deal with such a small matter, even if it is administrative.' Sometimes, of course, the question under dispute was such that the wisdom of Solomon could hardly have decided whether it was administrative or professional.

The CNR being one of the principal battlegrounds in this

departmental war of the frogs and the mice, it was not long before I started playing my own very minor part in the strategy. More important to me during the first few weeks of my service, however, were two quite non-official incidents, both of which stand out in vivid colours against the drab background of paper-littered desks, tall filing cabinets, and dimly-lit corridors.

Needing an envelope, I went across to the general office. It was the first time I had been there, and since the place was full of women and girls I naturally felt rather hesitant. Approaching the nearest desk I asked, 'Could you spare me an envelope?' (I pronounced the initial vowel of the word as a short 'e', as thought the syllable rhymed with 'hen').

'Oh, you mean an *awn*velope!' laughed the red-headed girl behind the desk, gaily handing me the controversial piece of stationery. I retreated in confusion.

The second incident occurred some time later. One lunch hour I wanted to consult the index of CNR members. The red-headed girl was alone in the office, reading a book. My heart thumped painfully. 'What are you reading?' I asked, to make conversation.

Instead of replying she blushed deeply and covered the open pages of the book with her two hands.

'Let me see,' I insisted, approaching her desk. Blushing more furiously still, she took away her hands and looked up at me in smiling confusion as I examined the book. It was Santayana's *Egotism in German Philosophy*. Her conquest of me was complete.

Sonia, as I was soon permitted to call her, was a medium-sized girl of twenty-two with strawberry blonde hair. Though not thin she was slightly built with small, undeveloped breasts. She had a heart-shaped face and a fair complexion. Her eyes were violet, nose perfectly shaped though slightly freckled, and mouth wide but not full. Next to her voice, the clearest and most musical I had ever heard, the most striking thing about her was the frank, generous, open expression of her face, on which I never saw even the slightest trace of ill-nature.

Whether derived from her Anglo-Irish father or her Franco-Russian mother there was, however, a marked strain of fecklessness in her make-up. Her stockings were laddered, her shoes dirty, her coat unbrushed, and she signed the late book more often than any other member of the staff. Later, when we were on confidential terms, she told me, with her usual frank gaiety of manner, 'I could never marry anyone with less than five thousand a year. When Daddy was alive Mummy had that amount and she could *never* make both ends meet.' This confession did not come as a rebuff to any proposal of mine. She had been proposed to by an admirer earning, unfortunately, only two thousand a year. During the time I knew her she had, in fact, five suitors, one of whom proposed almost as often as he saw her. But as she seemed not particularly fond of any of these shadowy figures, speaking of them only with compassionate amusement, it never occurred to me to feel jealous.

The confession referred to belongs to a period much later than the incident of the book. Meanwhile I enjoyed cosy chats with her behind one of the big filing cabinets, where I helped her make the morning coffee and afternoon tea whenever it was her turn to perform this duty. None of the other girls, which whom I was soon on first-name terms, ever commented in my presence on what must have been obvious to them all. But Thelma's jealous eyes were always on Sonia and me, and she tried hard to make me flirt with her.

My own regular duty was to open the letters which, twice a day, a departmental messenger put into my 'in' basket. This was not such a simple task as it looked, for after a few weeks the Chief left it to me to decide which letters could be dealt with by the general office and which needed his personal attention. In the latter case I called for the case papers. This often led to friction between Miss Cook and Thelma.

Miss Cook, who had the nose of a bloodhound for missing papers, after an unsuccessful search through all the files would look over the tops of her spectacles at nobody in particular, and declare, 'They must be on somebody's desk.' The girls perfunctorily searched their desks for the missing papers. 'There are no papers, Miss Cook,' Thelma would say at last. 'She's a new case.'

'No, no!' Miss Cook would exclaim, becoming excited. 'I know the name. R.L.V. Smith. She came up seven months ago in connection with that Nicholson case. There *must* be some papers somewhere.'

'I tell you there are no papers, Miss Cook,' Thelma would retort angrily. 'She's a new case. Give her to me.'

But once convinced there were papers Miss Cook never gave up the search till they were found. For the rest of the day she would go about muttering, 'R.L.V. Smith, R.L.V. Smith. Now where can her papers be?' Several hours later the stillness of the general office would be rent by a triumphant cry: 'Here they are; she had them all the time!'

'Miss Cook, how dare you touch my desk!' Thelma would shout, breaking off from a personal telephone conversation that had already lasted an hour and a half. But Miss Cook, her chubby face wreathed in smiles, was already out of the door and streaking across the corridor to the Chief's office.

Thelma's un-cooperativeness was part of a deliberate policy. Just as Miss Gretton, with whom she was on the best of terms, constantly tried to usurp administrative functions, Thelma did her utmost to keep the whole work of the general office in her own hands, and the two women worked together. Their intention was to trap the Chief. Had the letter from R.L.V. Smith been handed over to Thelma she would have quietly attached it to the case papers hidden on her desk and gone with the whole correspondence to Miss Gretton. Between them the matter would have been settled, even though it might require an administrative decision, or involve a matter of principle.

If Miss Cook either wearied of her search or, convinced that she had made a mistake, returned the letter to me with the remark that there were no case papers, the Chief dealt with it on its own merits. Meanwhile Miss Gretton and Thelma, knowing that the letter had been received, would immediately take the very action it should have prevented. Later, when the muddle came to light, the Chief would be accused of taking action on a letter without reference to the previous correspondence and Miss Cook blamed for not making a thorough search for the case papers. Thus only Miss Cook's obstinacy stood between the Chief and disaster.

Once she pursued papers for three weeks. Even when the Chief, convinced that there could be no previous correspondence, ordered her to surrender the letter that put her on the trail, she defied him and went on with her search. The missing papers were eventually discovered when she ransacked Thelma's desk for the fourth time. Where they had been in the meantime no one ever knew.

Sometimes Thelma would try to draw a red herring across the trail. After detaching the more important correspondence, she returned the rest of the case papers to the file; but Miss Cook was rarely deceived, for she seemed to have a memory not only for every set of case papers but for each individual letter that had ever passed through her hands. Another ruse was to file case papers out of alphabetical order. This move Miss Cook countered by checking the entire contents of the box files, of which there were several hundred, at least once a week.

After the morning post had been opened and Miss Cook was hot on the scent, the Chief and I simply talked. In addition to official business, which occupied only part of our time, we discussed philosophy, religion, and literature. In those days the great Trollope revival was beginning to sweep the reading public, and the Chief was among its most ardent supporters. Rarely did he go out to lunch without one of the minor works of his favourite author tucked beneath his arm. Since fiction was the branch of literature which I had cultivated least, I was slightly scornful of this enthusiasm, and the merits and demerits of Trollope were vigorously debated between us. In an effort to convince him of the truth of my system, which was then Neo-Hegelian, I started writing, in the manner of Proclus's *On the One*, a series of theses. After the ninetieth thesis I gave up, entangled in my own ideas.

At ten o'clock came the usual pleasant interlude behind the filing cabinet in the general office, at the end of which I departed with three cups of coffee. As soon as he had gulped down his, the Chief would hitch up his cuffs and with a cheery remark to me tackle the contents of his 'in' basket with vigour. I followed his example. The lunch hour I usually spent in quest of second-hand books. After a hurried lunch at a cheap Italian restaurant, I hastened along York Street to my favourite shop, the proprietor of which always gave me a cordial welcome, for I was his best customer. I also patronized a stall in the Dip, a rather suspicious market area to which there was access from York Street through a long dark tunnel that reeked of stale beer. In between the brewers' drays one would occasionally descry human refuse in the form of decrepit prostitutes and drunkards, some of whom would hoarsely beg for a copper. From these lunch-hour expeditions I rarely returned without one or two newly purchased volumes, so that it was not long before Father had to order for me yet another bookcase.

The instant I re-entered the office, the Chief hastily donned hat and coat and dashed out with his latest Trollope, flinging at me as he went an admonition to 'hold the fort'. Hardly had his footsteps died away along the corridor than the door would open to Miss Cook, whose lunch hour coincided with mine. 'What do you *think?*' she would exclaim, 'I found those missing papers under ...' Whereupon I would have to listen to her latest adventures among the filing cabinets. Occasionally I was honoured by a visit from Miss Gretton, who once or twice dangled her legs over the edge of my desk and tried to look like a lorelei on a rock. Shorter than Miss Cook's, her visits were made with the object of ascertaining whether the Chief had overstayed his lunch hour. So it if was three o'clock, I had to be careful to observe that he had not left the office till two. Thus her plan of throwing out in front of the MOH a casual remark about his never returning before four o'clock would be frustrated.

The latter part of the afternoon was devoted to dictating letters. When the Chief was ready, I telephoned the typing pool and asked them to send someone along. If the stenographer who appeared a few minutes later happened to be about sixty, the Chief would acknowledge her greeting with a scowl and a grunt and plunge at once into his dictation. If she was sixteen (there were no intermediate age groups) he would exclaim, 'Hullo, we haven't seen you for a long time! How are you?' After the blushing miss had said that she was all right, thank you, and answered other questions of a personal nature, she would be asked if she was sure she was quite comfortable, whether the chair was not too hard or the table too low, or the light insufficient, after which, with many cheerful smiles, the day's dictation would begin.

On Saturday afternoons I crossed Westminster Bridge and walked through Whitehall and Trafalgar Square on my weekly pilgrimage to the bookshops in Charing Cross Road. Though attracted most of all by the second-hand bookstalls where poets could still be bought for sixpence and philosophers for a shilling, I also penetrated the more sophisticated establishments where beings of indeterminate age and sex, in velveteen trousers and with long hair, dispensed Marx and Freud, Dylan Thomas and D.H. Lawrence, at much higher prices.

With Charing Cross Road as my base, I explored Soho, the Strand, Leicester Square, Shaftesbury Avenue, and Piccadilly Circus. The whole of this area was then overrun with American troops. They lounged at street corners, leaned against public buildings, clung to the railings of latrines, and jigged and ambled along the pavements. So numerous were they that they outnumbered the civilian population five to one. Plump and soft with good living, sometimes obese, they stood or strolled with their hands in their pockets, caps askew, and tunic buttons undone. A passing officer would be saluted with a casual flip of the hand and a familiar 'Hiya, Joe!' Most of them had hanging on to them two or three little painted harlots, not professional prostitutes but 'enthusiastic amateurs' of fourteen or fifteen eager to sell their skinny adolescent bodies to any GI who would give them a 'good time'. In every street huge white-helmeted MPs, heavily armed, kept grim watch upon the corruption that seethed and bubbled around them.

Younger members of the LCC Staff Association occasionally organized Saturday afternoon lectures and debates. Though these functions attracted me much less strongly than the bookshops of Charing Cross Road, I yielded to the persuasions of a youth who worked farther down the corridor and attended two or three of them. This

115

same youth, who was an ardent Communist, had already lent me a textbook of Dialectical Materialism. 'What do you think of it?' he eagerly enquired when I returned the book. But my Neo-Hegelianism had been offended by the author's dogmatic assertion that Marx had found Hegel standing on his head and had set him on his feet. I therefore replied, 'I think it's Marx who is standing on his head, not Hegel.'

At my first Staff Association debate, which was on the motion 'India should be granted immediate independence,' I took an instant dislike to the Chairman, an angular, masculine young woman with a high bony forehead who obviously thought that she was well on her way to becoming chairman of the LCC. When, shortly afterwards, an attempt was made to draw me more deeply into such activities by inviting me to read a paper, I therefore chose the subject 'The Inferiority of Women', interlarding my address with copious extracts from my favourite Schopenhauer diatribes against the 'weaker' sex. After I had read my paper there was a stunned silence. No doubt those rather leftist young members of the Staff Association had never before heard anything so shamelessly reactionary. But they had nothing to say in rebuttal of my arguments. Next day I read the paper to Sonia, who, despite my entreaties, had not attended the meeting. She merely laughed and exclaimed, 'Oh you're mad, quite mad!'

That summer I spent a week at Besthorpe, the tiny Norfolk village in which Nana had been born and where Father had spent several years of his boyhood. It was my third visit, and I stayed in great-grandmother's thatched cottage, now occupied by Uncle Arthur, Auntie Dolly, and Cousin Ezalda. Though I made a trip to Norwich, where I visited the cathedral, the Castle Museum, and the tomb of Sir Thomas Browne, I spent the best part of my time writing letters to Sonia. These letters, the first and the last love letters I ever wrote, were long, literary, and idealistic. In one of them I compared my love to that of Dante for Beatrice. Both my aunt and my cousin were intensely curious to know the reason for this frantic epistolary activity, for I wrote twice a day; but for all their teasing the secret remained unrevealed.

What Sonia thought of my declarations I never knew. The courage I had felt at a safe distance of a hundred miles from my beloved evaporated in her presence. Sonia herself seemed afraid even to allude to the subject. Though she was gay, friendly, and charming as ever, she seemed nervous when we were alone together, as though apprehensive of a sudden violent demonstration of passion. Sometimes she looked at me with a pleading expression, like that of a rabbit fascinated by a snake. On all subjects other than the one we both avoided I talked to her with the frank egotism of the lover; told her my ideas and ideals, ambitions and aspirations. She listened with a smile, laughing whenever I said anything more than usually outrageous, but always with a strange, half-frightened look in her eyes. Her usual comment was, 'You're a genius, no doubt, but absolutely mad.'

Return to London meant, almost as much as a return to Sonia, a renewal of acquaintance with the bookshops of Charing Cross Road. Expanding my sphere of operations, I began penetrating into two or three little courts which opened from it on the right. In one of these I discovered the oriental bookshop which, though well known to all serious English students of Eastern philosophy and religion, had been until then unknown to me. Unlike the other bookshops with their sixpenny and shilling boxes on either side of a wide open door, it was an aloof, reserved, almost mysterious place. In a single box outside the empty window on the left were some damaged specimens of the lighter sort of theosophical literature. The window on the right contained expensive books on the occult sciences. The door between was shut fast. Only after I had several times stopped to thumb the damaged volumes did I venture inside. The interior of the shop was even less like that of a bookshop than the exterior. Through a door at the back of the shop could be seen an octogenarian gentleman, in very powerful spectacles, sitting at a desk. Above the mantelpiece behind him hung a life-size photograph of Mme Blavatsky.

At John Watkins, which thereafter I visited frequently, I bought the two books by which I have been most profoundly influenced. These were the *Diamond Sutra*, which I read first in Gemmell's then in Max Müller's translation, and the *Sutra of Wei Lang* (Hui Neng). If, when I read *Isis Unveiled*, I knew that I was not a Christian, when I read the *Diamond Sutra* I knew that I was a Buddhist. Though this book epitomizes a teaching of such rarefied sublimity that even Arahants, saints who have attained individual nirvana, are said to become confused and afraid when they hear it for the first time, I at once joyfully embraced it with an unqualified acceptance and assent. To me the *Diamond Sutra* was not new. I had known it and believed it and realized it ages before and the reading of the *Sutra* as it were awoke me to the existence of something I had forgotten. Once I realized that I was a Buddhist it seemed that I had always been one, that it was the most natural thing in the world to be, and that I had never been anything else. My experience of the *Sutra of Wei Lang*, which I read in the original Shanghai edition of Wong Mow Lam's translation, though taking place at a slightly lower level, was repeated with much greater frequency. Whenever I read the text I would be thrown into a kind of ecstasy. Basically, of course, the teaching of the two sutras is the same, though it cannot be denied that Wei Lang's doctrine of the identity of *prajna* and *samadhi*, Wisdom and Meditation, has been productive of much confusion of thought, not only in Far Eastern Zen circles, but in their modern Western counterparts.

The realization that I was a Buddhist came in the later summer or early autumn of 1942. At about the same period I had for the first time experiences of the type which are generally known as psychic. Whether these started before or after reading the *Diamond Sutra* I do not remember. The latter alternative is the more likely as, after a longer or shorter interval of time, a spiritual experience is often as it were echoed on the lower intellectual, emotional, or psychic, or even physical, plane. All these experiences, perhaps seven or eight in number, occurred in my office in County Hall, generally when I was alone. Without any warning a whole series of future events would suddenly unroll themselves like a cinematograph before me. These events, which I saw not with the physical eyes but with what the Buddhist tradition terms the 'divine eye', appeared as clear, vivid, and distinct as anything I had ever seen by normal means. They were always previsions of what would happen in my immediate surroundings from half an hour to one hour afterwards. I therefore knew in advance who would come into the office, how they would stand, what they would say. Never did anything foreseen fail to occur. Later, in India and elsewhere, I met a number of people, including Europeans, who were much concerned with the development of psychic powers. While such powers undoubtedly can be developed by anybody who is prepared to submit to the proper training and discipline, Buddhist tradition is unanimous in maintaining that the better course is to direct all one's energies to the attainment of enlightenment and to allow psychic powers to come, if they do come, of their own accord.

From the office I now often went straight to the theatre, having under the Chief's tuition developed a love for the stage which I never in the slightest degree felt for the screen. I saw, among other plays, *Ghosts, Hedda Gabler,* and *The Way of the World* at the Duke of York's, *The Master Builder* and *An Ideal Husband* at the Westminster, *Othello* at Wimbledon, and *Twelfth Night* and *Lady Precious Stream* at the Open Air Theatre at Regent's Park. But more deeply than by any of these dramas was I moved by Leslie French's ballet *Everyman.* Though I had read the old morality play several years before, along with *The Fall of Lucifer* and *The Harrowing of Hell,* it now struck me with the force of a thunderbolt. Perhaps for the first time in my life I realized that Friends and Kin, Wealth and Possessions, must all be left behind, and that only our Good Deeds can go with us when Death summons us to make our last journey. So deeply was I impressed that when I tried to write an appreciation of *Everyman* I found my feelings too strong for expression. What, then, would have been the effect of this drama on the unsophisticated audiences of the Age of Faith to whom it was staged, not as an evening's entertainment, but as part of a religious ritual! Only in Tibetan Buddhist literature did I ever again hear that thrilling note of intense pathos, of direct, naked sincerity of religious utterance—so different from the sanctimonious tones of conventional piety—which reverberates through *Everyman.*

With the growth of my interest in the Wisdom of the East visits to, and purchases from, John Watkins became more and more frequent. To the study of Buddhism was annexed that of Taoism and Confucianism, Hinduism and Islam, Sufism and Christian mysticism. My enjoyment of literature was enriched by the discovery of Chinese and Persian poetry, in both of which fields I read as widely as my dependence on translations allowed. Next to Buddhism I was most attracted by Taoism, and among the Taoist classics it was the *Tao Teh King* for which I conceived the strongest admiration. This wonderful distillation of concentrated spiritual wisdom I read in six or eight translations, gaining from each one a new appreciation of its inexhaustible riches of meaning. To me the best translation was Chu Ta Kao's, which moreover led me, via an advertisement on its back cover, straight to *The Middle Way* and eventually to the London Buddhist Society.

After becoming a subscriber to this journal, which I read with avidity, I wrote two articles on Buddhism. In view of the way in which I subsequently emphasized that our basic allegiance should be not to this or that school, but to the whole Buddhist tradition, it is significant that the first of these articles was entitled 'The Unity of Buddhism'. The second, which was too long to be published, dealt with the doctrine of Dependent Origination, otherwise known as Conditioned Co-production—another major preoccupation of later years. Clare Cameron, the editor of *The Middle Way*, had already written to say that she was glad to welcome a new subscriber so well versed in Buddhism, which kind words I did not really deserve. To her, therefore, the articles were submitted. The letter which I wrote on this occasion gave rise to a correspondence which has continued, despite interruptions, down to the present.

In the spring Sonia was called up. We parted, as we had met, in the general office. With the intention of allowing the rest of the staff time to depart, I had waited for a few minutes after office hours before crossing the corridor for our last minutes together. To my dismay Thelma was still at her desk. As though in mockery of the look of chagrin which must have appeared on my face, she called out, with pretended archness, 'If you want me to leave the room you'll have to carry me out in your arms!' Never had I so hated a woman. Ignoring her, I turned to Sonia, and after a few minutes of ordinary talk, during which my eyes were eloquent of all the love, desperation, and anguish my tongue was prevented from uttering, we parted with mutual good wishes and a conventional handshake. Thelma's jealous eyes watched us closely from over the filing baskets and followed me to the door.

Hardly knowing what I did, I boarded the homeward tram at the foot of Westminster Bridge and sat on top with grief more acute than I had yet known clutching at my heart. At Clapham Common I suddenly decided to alight. For several months I had been aware of growing estrangement between Mother and Father and instinctively I shrank from returning in a state of such black and bitter sorrow to a home where the peace and consolation I needed were no longer to be found. Instead, like some stricken beast returning to its hole to die, I took refuge in the familiar premises of the second-hand bookshop.

Exactly two hours later, by the clock tower at the tram stop, I emerged. As I boarded the Tooting Broadway tram I realized, with a shock of astonishment, that during the whole of that time I had not once thought of Sonia. Yet though, as it seemed, Nature had not meant me for a lover, I never forgot her. From the letters which came from the ATS training camp to which she had been posted I learned that though well she was unhappy. But that her unhappiness had the same cause as mine she gave me no reason to believe.

Summer passed quickly, and with it my last season as a civilian. After a holiday at Torquay with Joan, who had taken her School Certificate and now lived at home, I was called for my final medical examination. To my amazement I was classified B2. 'There's nothing wrong with your heart,' declared the cardiologist to whom, in view of my history, I had been sent by the general board.

'But I was in bed for two years!' I protested, outraged. With a slight frown he again applied his stethoscope to my chest and back. 'Absolutely nothing wrong,' he repeated, after an examination which seemed to me even more perfunctory than the first. 'Your heart's perfectly sound.'

I left the hospital in bewilderment, not knowing whether to feel delighted at this sudden revelation that I was not a semi-convalescent, but a healthy young man, or dismayed at the prospect of being conscripted. Father was at first equally astonished, but after discussing this unexpected development we agreed that the permanent advantage of good health more than outweighed the temporary inconvenience of a year to two in the army. Consequently we went to the public house where Father now spent most of his evenings and celebrated the news with several rounds of drinks.

My only worry was the thought that I might not be able to finish the novel on which I had been working since the middle of September. So, giving up other interests, I spent all my weekends and evenings shut in my room, where I rapidly filled notebook after notebook. Poetry, of course, could not be so easily relinquished. Ever since joining the LCC I had composed poems in tram and tube while travelling between Tooting Broadway and Westminster. Those composed during the morning journey were written down as soon as I arrived at the office; those composed during the evening journey as soon as I reached home.

One October evening, while I was hanging up my hat and coat in the hall, I heard Father's voice calling me from the sitting-room. Alarmed by his unusual agitation I sprang to the open door. Father was standing in the middle of the carpet with an almost berserk expression on his face. Mother sat quietly weeping; near her sat Sid, looking glum and uncomfortable. Joan was sobbing with her head on the mantelpiece.

'Your mother wants to leave us!' Father burst out, before I had time to realize the terrible significance of the scene.

Now that the worst had happened, I knew that I had

been expecting it for a long time; but I did not know what to say.

'Do you want to see your mother again!' Father demanded of Joan with unusual roughness.

'No, no, I never want to see her again!' replied my poor sister with renewed sobs. She had been at home only two months and for her the blow had fallen without warning.

Mother began to sob as if her heart would break, wailing, 'Oh, don't talk like that, dear!' But Joan only repeated her words with greater vehemence.

Turning to me, Father asked, 'Do *you* want to see your mother again?' His tone suggested that I could give no other reply than Joan's. Moistening my lips with my tongue, I replied, 'Yes, of course I do.' At these words both Mother and Joan sobbed more violently than ever.

'Well,' said Father, slightly taken aback, 'I won't stand in your way.' Even in anger he was a just man.

How the miserable scene ended I do not know. Sid, who was acquainted with Father, having visited the house several times, tried to make amends at his departure by saying, 'I can't say how sorry I am that this has happened.' But these humble words were of no more avail then the falling of a drop of water upon a red-hot iron plate.

For the rest of the evening we sat in wretched silence. At nine o'clock Joan kissed Father with a bright 'Goodnight, Dad!' and walked out of the room past Mother without a word. Mother's face, whiter and more miserable than I had ever known it, smote me to the heart. After bidding Father goodnight I therefore went over to her and kissed her with a 'Goodnight, Mum!' as usual.

The next few weeks were the worst I had ever known. Three times Mother tried to leave and three times she broke down at the last minute and was unable to go. The ties of twenty-four years were not so easily broken. The intervals between these attempts were periods of unprecedented strain for all of us. Mother was terrified that Father would commit suicide. Once, on my return from the office, I found her sitting at the bottom of the stairs almost crazy with apprehension. From the kitchen I could hear the sound of Father's feet as he paced like a madman up and down the room.

'What's the matter?' I asked. But Mother was becoming hysterical, and she could only repeat, in a whisper, 'Go in to him, go in to him', in a manner that chilled my blood.

Softly opening the door, I asked, 'Are you all right, Dad?' Father stopped pacing and sat down wearily, passing his hand across his brow. 'Yes, it's all right now, son', he replied quietly.

Wherever Father went I accompanied him, for Mother would plead, 'Don't leave him. He might do himself an injury.' Usually we went to the public house, where Father drank heavily, and where, to keep him company, I drank heavily too. At night I lay in bed anxiously listening to Mother's and Father's voices as they talked downstairs. Whenever one of them was raised, however slightly, my heart thumped with fear. Only when I heard Mother coming upstairs to her room in the early hours of the morning would I be able to sleep. However, as the weeks went by they talked more and more quietly, as though what had happened was a burden they both had to bear. Then one Saturday afternoon I came home from the office to find that Mother had gone.

At the end of November, a few days after the novel had been finished, came my calling-up papers.

9. The Misfit

Leatherhead, where the Signals Unit to which I had been instructed to report was stationed, was a quiet old-fashioned country town in the heart of Surrey. As we approached the crossroads on the far side of the town the traffic lights abruptly changed from green to red. Ernie, the ginger-haired Cockney who had travelled down with me, remarked how odd it was that a town with no traffic should need traffic lights. We were both more than a little nervous. Turning left past the cinema, as a friendly police-man had directed, we passed a field and a row of small houses. Next came a hospital which I recognized as one of those to which the CNR allocated nurses. Before we could reach the end of the road the November rain, which had been threatening all the morning, started falling steadily. Despite our reluctance we quickened our pace and, passing the remaining villas, turned right into a country lane. After a dozen yards the land became a cart-track and we were ankle deep in mud. Perhaps we had lost our way! After anxious consultations we pressed on between the tall hedges until, turning a bend, we saw a khaki-clad figure standing on guard beside a gate.

An hour later, feeling very conspicuous in our civilian suits, we were seated at a scrubbed wooden table in the dining hall, with about forty other men, eating sausages and mash, followed by apple pie and custard. 'Grub doesn't seem too bad in this hole', muttered Ernie, busy with a second helping of pie. But the sight and smell of the tubs of greasy water in which we afterwards washed our plates outside almost made me vomit.

The camp was both small and new. It consisted of an eight-roomed house, obviously requisitioned, and two rows of army huts, some still under construction, that had been laid out in the grounds to one side of the house. The dining hall, which faced the huts, was built alongside the house and communicated with the back door of the kitchen. To the left of the huts, in view of the gate, stood the structure we soon learned to refer to as 'the ablutions'. The trampling of army boots had left no trace of the garden, and in between the huts, as well as between the huts and the house, were avenues of mud. The camp was surrounded by six feet of barbed wire.

In the afternoon Ernie and I were issued with uniforms which did not fit, boots which felt too large, and rifles which seemed much too heavy to lift, together with sundry other articles for which we did not think we would have any particular use. My hair, rather long by army standards, was cut. We were then taken to a hut containing a dozen army cots, two of which were unoccupied, and told that we belonged to 'C' squad and were to take orders from the corporal in charge.

For the next three weeks I felt as though my soul was petrified. Thought, emotion, and will were suspended. I carried out my duties and obeyed orders mechanically, without any mental reaction. It was as though the integrity of my inner being could be safeguarded only by means of a temporary paralysis that not only prevented it from reacting to army life but made it impossible for army life to act upon or influence it in any way. Had this defensive mechanism not come into operation the futility of the existence into which I had been so abruptly plunged might have driven me mad.

Our day began at five o'clock. Still half asleep, we stumbled from the huts and through the darkness towards the light that fell through the door of 'the ablutions'. Unless we arrived very early it was necessary to queue up for our wash and shave, as the number of taps was limited. Porridge and poached eggs were eaten as dawn broke. The rest of our time until parade was spent making up beds for inspection, polishing brasses, applying green blanco to webbing, and cleaning rifles. At eight o'clock we fell in outside the house. After the RSM had run his eye over our rather straggling line, the two corporals were given their orders. With a sudden change of manner from the obsequious to the bullying, they turned smartly from the RSM to their respective squads, barked out a command, and marched us off to the strip of newly asphalted road which was our parade ground.

These drill periods were a nightmare. Had we been allowed simply to march, the foot drill with which we started would not have proved difficult to learn. But apparently intimidation was the army method. We were bawled at for not holding our heads high enough or swinging our arms high enough or sticking our chests out far enough. The main principle of the drill seemed to be that what the squad did was always wrong. One morning an elderly recruit, formerly a teacher, became so exasperated by the corporal's constant hectoring that he snapped, 'It's no use you shouting at me like that, my man, I'm doing my best!' But bad as foot drill was, rifle drill, which we started a week later, was far worse, and our new instructor a fiend compared to short, fresh-complexioned Corporal Smith.

Corporal Halford was a small, ape-like Welshman whose habit it was to masturbate in front of the inmates of his hut every night before going to bed. His manner was

simultaneously oily and ferocious, his expression somewhere between a leer and a snarl. It was his practice to
threaten the squad with detention, pack drill, fatigues, and
other punishments in a low, menacing tone and then
suddenly startle it with a command that cracked like a
whiplash. The threats were supposed to reduce us to such
a state of nervousness that when the command came we
jumped. By this method he certainly put a finer polish on
our foot drill. But his efforts to teach us rifle drill only
reduced the squad to suppressed laughter and himself to
snarling ferocity. One of the recruits was a bald-headed
businessman who, since a uniform could not be found to
fit him, was still wearing black jacket and pin-stripe
trousers. 'I'm so sorry, corporal', he said with a giggle one
morning, 'I just can't seem to manage the bloody thing.'

He spoke for most of us. The rifles were not only large
and heavy but extremely difficult to handle. The smallest
recruit, in fact, asked the RSM if he could have a shorter
weapon. It would be hard to say whose astonishment was
the greater, the RSM's at this strange request or the little
recruit's on learning that rifles were all the same size. 'Just
like the army', he grumbled, 'they might as well give us all
the same size boots.'

Bad as the rest of the squad was at rifle drill, Ernie and
I were far worse. As we often remarked to each other,
ability to handle a rifle seemed in inverse ratio to one's IQ.

In the afternoon, Corporal Smith, who was in charge of
our hut, taught us 'naming the parts of the rifle.' Unfortunately he was unable to pronounce certain sounds. 'Male
thread', for example, was always 'male tread.' At first we
carefully reproduced all his mispronunciations. He also
taught us how to take the rifle apart for cleaning, how to
use the pull-through, and how to load and unload. Next
to striking an officer, we gathered, the most serious offence
one could commit in the army was to lose one's rifle.

Every other afternoon we had an hour's PT on the lawn behind the house. These periods I was soon able to evade. The gruff old MO who had inoculated us had merely said, 'If you collapse during PT fall out and report sick!' But thinking it safer to fall out first I told the corporal I had been excused PT on medical grounds. When there was nothing else to do, we were ordered into our jeans for fatigues. This we liked best of all. Ernie and I quickly discovered that provided we carried something in our hand and walked past NCOs with a brisk, purposeful air, we were never molested. Many an afternoon did we spend walking about the camp with the same piece of wood or the same empty bucket.

Unless we happened to be confined to barracks, our evenings were our own. Ernie and I could not escape from camp quickly enough. Usually we went into Leatherhead immediately after tea and spent the evening in the Forces Canteen. On the way back to camp I sometimes telephoned Mother, who was then living at Clapham.

But the best part of the day was the hour or two before lights out. With the beds made down and the mouth of the stove glowing fiery red, the bleak bare hut looked almost comfortable. In twos or threes our fellow inmates re-turned, most of them redder in the face, louder of voice, and more uncertain of step than when they went out. Lying or sitting on our beds, or on our neighbours' beds, we talked and laughed in the warm, friendly, uninhibited atmosphere of the barrack room until our 'personalities', that had been crushed flat by the corporal's boots all day, began to revive, and our individual idiosyncrasies to bloom like exotic flowers.

Ernie, who at first occupied the bed adjacent to mine, had naturally become my best friend. A month younger than I, he did not look more than fourteen. Despite the sharpness of his features his face wore an expression of such guilelessness and innocence that even the hearts of NCOs were touched. He was, however, by far the shrewdest person in the whole camp and on more than one occasion was I staggered by the almost supernatural quality of his cunning. The hut soon discovered that he possessed a pair of well-developed breasts, the fame whereof spread throughout the camp and reached even the Colonel's ears. At first Ernie was very ashamed of these features, scowling whenever they were made the subject of comment. But he quickly learned that they could be turned to advantage. More than one of our married friends was deeply disturbed at the sight of Ernie sitting on the end of his bed playing with his shapely white breasts. Not that he had the slightest intention of granting any favours. 'Don't go away,' he would mutter out of the corner of his mouth, whenever any of his admirers showed signs of becoming too importunate. 'That dirty bugger's after me again.'

Four of the other inmates of the hut were of our own age. Laurie, a calm, smiling, good-natured boy with a slight squint, preferred to go about alone. Alice, so called after a famous actress whose surname was the same as his own, was distinguished by his ability to drop off to sleep at a moment's notice at any time in any position. A fat, owlish youth, his pulse rate was thirty-two, the lowest of which I ever heard. Mike, clean-limbed and handsome, found it impossible to adapt himself to army life. At first defiant and disobedient, he eventually became openly rebellious and in the end got into very serious trouble. He was the type the army breaks. Smeed, who arrived later and whom we never called by his first name, was a slow, moon-faced youth much interested in railway engines who was neither liked nor disliked.

The idiosyncrasies of our elders, having had in some cases twice as much time for development, were naturally more marked. Pinkie, the schoolmaster who had snapped at Corporal Smith, was never seen off parade without his pipe. His hobby was collecting bus and tram routes; his favourite reading, timetables. He knew, stop by stop, the route of every bus and tram in London and the Home Counties. To him a holiday meant a ride over one of the longer and less familiar routes.

Batty Tatty, or Tat—undersized, weedy, and pimpled— had a loud voice and the music hall type of Lancashire accent. He spent the whole of every evening deeply absorbed in a large album which contained only photographs of himself from the age of two months up- wards. A strange combination of simplicity and cunning, he was utterly selfish, and though the butt of all, became the friend of none. Harry 'the Ticker', who had asked the RSM for a shorter rifle, was so called for his constant cheerful grumble, which was so incessant as to resemble the regular ticking of a watch. He and Alice apparently had an elective affinity for each other, for they were always together. Fish, a Jew of uncertain age, took himself so seriously as to become an object of ridicule. His greatest fear was that he might have to cut short his black, wavy hair, which was thin on top and dyed; his greatest sorrow, when he was made to hand in his greatcoat after having it altered by his tailor. Pete and Eddie were even more inseparable than most chums. The former was the fattest, the latter the tallest and thinnest, inmate of the hut. Though very obviously himself an Anglo-Indian, Eddie always spoke of 'the bloody wogs' with contempt and loathing. Behind his back the hut was unimpressed. 'He's a bloody wog himself,' we chuckled.

The hut's chief topic of conversation was sex. Ernie and I and the rest of the youngsters, who had nothing of our own to contribute, listened while the older men discussed the size, shape, and mechanics of their respective organs, their sexual experiences, the different modes of copulation, and the sexual physiology of the female, all in the most exhaustive detail. But once our natural curiosity was satisfied, we found this incessant preoccupation with sex both boring and disgusting and turned away to discuss more interesting subjects among ourselves.

In the course of my fourth week at camp my numbed faculties began to revive. For some days I had been composing Persian-style quatrains as we marched up and down our parade ground. These poems, more than three hundred of which were eventually written down, came up crocus-like through the crust of despair that overlaid my heart. The current of my inner life, frozen ice-hard since the day I joined the army, thawed and began to flow. As a mountain stream discovers a path round the boulders it is powerless to displace, I awoke to the fact that, although military life might for a time divert, it could not permanently deflect, the master current of my being. Though it could waste my time, it could not destroy my interests. I resolved I would allow the army neither to make me or break me. Since it was stronger than I, I would observe its ridiculous regulations and obey the orders of its idiotic minions, but with all the strength and integrity of my soul I would loathe, despise, and utterly repudiate the army and all it stood for.

The nature of our unit eventually made it easy for me not only to carry out this resolution but actively to pursue my own interests. Full-time military training had quickly yielded to half-time, the mornings or afternoons thus gained being devoted to learning Morse. The 'technical' corporals who now took us in hand were notoriously indifferent to matters of discipline, and between them and the 'military' corporals smouldered ill-concealed hostility. Corporal Smith left our hut to take charge of a new intake, his place being occupied by Tom, a handsome young giant of a technical instructor whom Ernie's breasts at once captivated. After our return from Christmas leave drill and fatigues were discontinued, and after a fierce battle between the technical and military NCOs we were even excused guard duties.

The arrival of a Regular Army sergeant seemed at first to augur trouble. He did, indeed, inveigle the CO, a former bank manager, into ordering a company parade in full marching order. But the sight of us lined up outside in the lane with our packs askew and our rifles at different angles was so ludicrous that the experiment was not repeated. Besides, the technical side was reinforced by the arrival of a fat, friendly CSM and a small, grizzled, blasphemous QM, who lounged about in canvas shoes with their hands in their pockets, buttons undone and without caps. Though their informal presence soon made it obvious that our duties would not be military in the narrow sense of the term at all, the Unit's indispensable minimum of Regular Army NCOs did their utmost to make camp life conform to the traditional pattern.

From the point of view of the work we did later, our being in the army was an accident. Nothing the military NCOs taught us proved of the slightest value. Packs and rifles proved mere impedimenta. Futile exhibitions of Regular Army infantilism such as company parades wasted time that should have been devoted to improving our knowledge of the work to which our country had called us. The officers and the RSM, of course, knew this long before we did, and the very perfunctory military routine they had included in our training was no more than a token recognition of the fact that the unit was part of the army. Yet to the last we were harassed by pettifogging Regular NCOs who made life as difficult for us as they possibly could.

Corporal Halford's behaviour over the question of leave

was a case in point. After a few of us, including Ernie and myself, had twice or thrice gone home on weekend passes, he warned us, as though in friendly confidence, that the RSM strongly objected to this, and that those who offended in future would be transferred to the Signals Depot in Oswestry, a name as dreadful to our ears as that of Sheol to the ancient Hebrews. This information disturbed us profoundly. The married men saw their opportunities for sexual intercourse curtailed. Ernie and I and the rest of the youngsters felt that without an occasional brief spell of freedom our existence would be intolerable. For several days the inmates of every hut debated the subject with gloomy faces. Some felt Halford's warning had saved us from disaster; others that he was bluffing; most, that it would be better not to take any chances. That weekend nearly everybody remained in camp. Ernie and I uneasily went home as usual.

Not long afterwards the RSM held a question and answer meeting. NCOs were excluded. Halford, however, was kind enough to warn us against asking questions about leave. After the RSM had answered innocuous enquiries about promotions, widow's pensions, and medical treatment, one long-suffering married man, greatly daring, rose to his feet and hesitantly asked the question which was uppermost in our minds: 'How often should we apply for a weekend pass?'

'As often as you like', replied the RSM. 'In fact,' he continued crisply, 'unless you happen to be on guard duty I would advise you to apply every week. Now that you've started your technical training you'll naturally be feeling a bit of a strain. After a day or two at home you'll come back to your duties all the fresher. No need for anyone to be in camp at weekends except the guard.'

The technical training, then recently begun, had in fact proved a considerable strain on almost all the older men.

For some, the learning of the Morse code was in itself difficult enough. (Ernie had learned it in the Boy Scouts, I in the BB.) But that was merely a beginning. As we gradually progressed from receiving at a speed of five words a minute to a speed of ten, and from ten to fifteen, several, unable to stand the increase of nervous tension, fell by the wayside and were transferred to general duties. Ernie and I, who soon led the class, long afterwards ruefully agreed that it would have been better for us to have fallen too. For whereas throw-outs who worked in the office were eventually promoted NCOs and WOs, we remained signalmen for ever. But in those early days, not knowing what was in store, we zealously pursued the path of our own undoing.

Stimulated by the encouragement of Tom and the officers, our speed steadily increased, and we were soon far ahead of the rest of the class. Though each did his best to surpass the other, we invariably passed our speed tests together. Our enthusiasm was largely due to consciousness of our enhanced prestige. The last in the drill squad had become the first in the technical class. The despair of the Regular Army corporals were the delight of the Morse instructors. When, one afternoon, we both blocked for one minute at a speed of thirty-one, faster than which even Tom could not transmit, we felt that our theory that the worse you were at squad drill the greater was your intelligence had been fully vindicated.

Meanwhile spring had come. The laburnums we passed on our way in to town had burst into yellow flame, while the young leaves of the copper-beech trees showed a chocolate-veined redness against the late afternoon sky. Ever sensitive to change of season, but most of all to the advent of spring, I felt strangely exhilarated. Since our promotion to the Set Room, whence for security reasons all but the instructors and operators were strictly barred, we enjoyed more weekend passes and afternoons off than

ever. Father, always pleased to see me home again, joc-
osely remarked that in *his* army days leave had not been
so easy to get. Mother seemed to spend Saturday afternoons waiting behind the front door of her flat, for it
always flew open even before I had finished ringing.
Though more subdued than before, she seemed happy and
contented. She and Father had agreed on a divorce. With
Sid, who sometimes came to tea, my relations were cordial,
for it was impossible not to like the quiet, friendly, inof-
fensive man. Joan, too, now reconciled to Mother and on
good terms with Sid, was also a frequent visitor. Tall and
well developed, she worked in a bank; but her ambition,
of which Father heard with dismay, was to join the ATS.
Sometimes I went to see Nana and Auntie Noni, on one
occasion spending the afternoon rambling with Auntie
over Wimbledon Common, where mile after mile the
purple-black heather showed patches of tender green,
while along the edges of the wood fern-shoots stood
among last year's yellow-brown bracken like little green
croziers.

Our evenings Ernie and I usually spent in the crowded
bar of the King's Head with Tom, who taught us to drink
black-and-tans but took good care we did not have too
many. Sometimes we wrote letters and played table-tennis
with the ATS in the Forces Recreation Room in the High
Street. Once or twice I took Ernie to Ewell, only two or
three stations along the line. Auntie Kath, who had returned from Torquay with Uncle Charles after the Blitz,
was friendly and voluble as ever. On learning that she had
herself cooked us scrambled eggs and chipped potatoes
the rest of the family was dumbfounded. 'Were they eat-
able?' I was asked in obvious disbelief.

One Saturday afternoon Ernie and I climbed to the top
of Box Hill. Far below us tiny fields of different shades of
green and brown made a patchwork to the horizon,

gradually softening into haze. In between were hedges, trees, and farms. Here and there a pond flashed molten gold in the sun. Just below the horizon showed the dark smudge of towns. As we lay in the hot grass, the earth as it were lifting us up to the embraces of the sun which swam in a great sky of cloudless blue, I read a few chapters of *Thus Spake Zarathustra*. Intoxicated by those ardent words, I wanted to shout them out in the face of the sun so that they might echo from end to end of the sky. But after shutting my eyes for a minute against the blinding brilliance of the light, I saw they were already written in quivering scarlet letters across the blue.

In Leatherhead my favourite spot was the garden of a teashop. Blackbirds, bright-eyed and yellow-billed, hopped on the lawn, and pink and white petals drifted from the fruit-trees on to the pages of my book. I was reading at the time, with equal delight, Donne and Herrick. An unusually felicitous line went through me like a spear. Sometimes, closing the book, I would fall into a muse and try to shape the rhythms and the images that were ringing in my head into verses of my own. Later, on the outskirts of the town, I discovered a mile or two of river, overhung with willows, up and down which kingfishers flashed crimson and blue. Sitting beside the shallow, sunlit water, at the bottom of which sticks and stones were clearly visible, I read *The Middle Way*, in which my article 'The Unity of Buddhism' had appeared a few months earlier.

Having learned about its activities, and seen my name in the pages of its journal, I was naturally desirous of coming into closer contact with the London Buddhist Society. One warm Saturday afternoon, therefore, I found my way to the rooms it then occupied over a restaurant in Great Russell Street. I had finished looking at the books and was talking to the librarian when in came a pixie-like figure with a square-cut fringe and voluminous tweed cloak. This was Clare Cameron. When I introduced myself to her she was astonished at seeing a boy instead of the middle-aged man she had imagined. For my part, I recognized in her one of those rare spirits who, in the words of the Indian poet, are tender as a flower and hard as a diamond. I liked her instantly. After she had introduced me to the founder-president, Christmas Humphreys, a correct gentlemanly figure in a lounge suit, a recording of Bach's 'Sheep May Safely Graze' was played and the meeting began.

Thereafter I attended meetings as often as I could. Usually not more than a dozen people were present. One afternoon an air raid warning sounded while we were meditating, for in a last desperate bid for victory, before the final crash, Germany had started its indiscriminate launching of V1s against the civilian population of London and the Home Counties. But either out of Buddhist equanimity or British phlegm we continued to meditate, not stirring even when, a few minutes later, the windows rattled with the blast of an explosion.

Among the members with whom I became acquainted was R.L. Jackson, a short grizzled man in sports jacket and baggy flannels who had obviously had a hard life and whose conversation, like his writings, was larded with quotations from the English poets. It seemed odd that he should address the president deferentially as 'Mr Humphreys' when the latter called him simply 'Jackson', treating him in an off-hand, patronizing sort of manner. Perhaps I had assumed that class distinctions would not be recognized within in the Society. Nearer my own age was Arnold Price, with whom I could discuss Buddhism more freely than with anybody else. One evening we progressed, arguing, through every public house between Great Russell Street and Waterloo Station—perhaps not the most seemly behaviour for either the future translator of *The Diamond Sutra* or the future bhikshu.

A more Buddhistic occasion was that on which Humphreys took us all to a vegetarian restaurant for dinner, in the course of which he gave an amusing description of how he had tried to translate one of his own poems into French. Clare Maison, whom I took part of the way home afterwards, was like most of the women members a great admirer of the president. As we stood on the draughty tube platform waiting for her train, she told me about her efforts to collect material for a biography of Ananda Maitreya, the first Englishman to return to England as a bhikshu.

By this time I was sufficiently adjusted to life in the Unit to be able to pursue my study of Buddhism unperturbed by the un-Buddhistic surroundings. The books I borrowed from the Society's library I usually read sitting on the quiet banks of the river, where I also wrote two or three poems afterwards published in *The Middle Way*. Memories of *The Systems of Buddhistic Thought* and *Thirty Stanzas on Representation Only*, both of which influenced me deeply, are inseparably connected with those of dragonflies, gauze-winged and sapphire-bodied, delicately poised on the surface of the water, over which played reflections and shadows of willow leaves. This was perhaps as it should have been. Was not the Buddha-nature reflected in every natural object, in every flower and stone and blade of grass?

Back in the Set Room I pondered on the new, yet strangely familiar, teachings with which I was gradually becoming acquainted. Sometimes, neglecting my task of intercepting unidentifiable transmissions, I sat with headphones over my ears, hands resting on the dials, and simply gazed out of the window at the sky. At the end of every hour I wrote 'Nil to report' in the log before me. On the lawn outside a new intake practised charging with fixed bayonets at a dummy on which the heart and stomach were indicated by red patches. The sergeant was satisfied with their performance only when, with rage-distorted features and bloodcurdling yells, they rushed like madmen upon the dummy and eviscerated it with gleeful ferocity.

In May the Buddhist Society celebrated, as it did every year, the full moon day of the Indian month of Vaishakha, anniversary of the Birth, Enlightenment, and Parinirvana of Gautama the Buddha. The meeting must have been held on a Saturday or a Sunday afternoon, for I was able to attend. Mother, who had been studying some elementary books on Buddhism, accompanied me. As we sat at the back of the hall waiting for the meeting to begin, a short stout gentleman of Mongolian appearance, in a dark suit and carrying an attaché case, entered the hall and disappeared into an adjoining room. Five minutes later he reappeared in orange robes. This was U Thittila, the first Buddhist monk I had seen. Later, when I was myself 'in the robes', I heard that narrowly-formalistic Burmese Buddhists had severely criticized him for his supposed misconduct in wearing ordinary European clothes when not actually performing his religious duties. English Buddhists saw the matter in quite a different light. Throughout the Blitz U Thittila had worked as a stretcher-bearer, on several occasions risking his life to rescue people trapped beneath fallen masonry. Finding that the voluminous drapery of his robes hampered his movements he sensibly exchanged them for more practical garments. People who knew him said he practised what he preached. I have always been glad that it was from him that I first took the Three Refuges and Five Precepts, with the recitation of which the meeting opened, U Thittila intoning them in Pali and Humphreys leading the responses. At the end of the meeting I introduced Mother to Humphreys and Clare Cameron, both of whom were among the speakers. U Thittila, again in his dark suit, hurried away. The V1s were still falling and he most likely had a job to do.

A few days later Clare Cameron invited me to have tea with her at her Bloomsbury flat. On the way up to the bright pleasant kitchen I caught a glimpse of her husband, Thomas Burke, at work in his book-lined study. If at our first meeting she had impressed me as being tender *and* hard, I now saw that Clare appeared not only very young but very old—a combination of elf and sibyl. Her physical age might have been anywhere between thirty and fifty. But what struck me most was the way in which her whole face lit up from within when she smiled—lit up through a faint network of tiny lines and wrinkles that testified that, for her, understanding had not been achieved without suffering. She looked frail as gossamer. But I soon realized that she was the only person in the society with enough strength of character not to be dominated by Humphreys.

In the course of my first visit she gave me a copy of her book of poems *A Stranger Here*. A week or two later, taking my courage in both hands, I showed her what I thought were the best of my own verses. As we walked through Kensington Gardens she gave me the benefit of some very sound criticism. Ten years later, when I published *Messengers From Tibet and Other Poems*, I dedicated it to her in token of my gratitude and admiration.

Several times that June, as I sat twiddling knobs and dials in the Set Room, I saw the black cigar-like shape of a V1 streaking through the sky in the direction of London. Once, watching one of these sinister objects, I heard the engine cut off and saw it suddenly nose-dive into a field. The explosion that followed rattled the windows. But dangerous as I knew them to be I little thought that one of them would be responsible for the destruction of my own home.

After leaving camp at one o'clock on Saturday afternoon as usual, I alighted from the tram at the bottom of our road at two-thirty. It was one of those bright, clear summer days which make a disaster seem all the more horrible in contrast, as if Nature cared nothing for the misery of man. As I stepped on to the pavement I noticed that tiles were missing from the roofs of several houses and a few windows broken. Obviously a 'rocket' had fallen somewhere near. As I climbed the hill the damage became worse. Whole roofs had been blown off and hardly a pane of glass was intact. Our own house was still out of sight round the bend at the top of the road. Fear gripped my heart, but I did not quicken my pace. The house only three or four doors down from ours was half destroyed. Several people stared at me curiously as I passed. Turning the bend I saw, to my intense relief, Father standing outside the gate in conversation with a neighbour. His bicycle was propped against the kerb. Behind him the whole front of the house gaped open; the downstairs ceiling sagged dangerously.

'Seems rather badly damaged,' I remarked. 'When did it happen?'

'About an hour ago,' Father replied quite cheerfully. 'The dust was still settling when I arrived.'

'Where were you at the time, then?'

'Oh, I had just stopped at Jack and Hilda's on my way back from work, just to see if they were all right. As soon as I heard the explosion I jumped on my bike and came here.'

Had Father returned at one o'clock, as he usually did on Saturdays, instead of at one-thirty, he would surely have been killed, as the rocket had exploded on our very doorstep, where the dent it had made was later found. Father's anxiety about the safety of my uncle and aunt had saved his life. Mother was, of course, at Clapham; Joan had joined the ATS three weeks previously. Had Mother not left us, had Father not returned late, had Joan not joined the ATS, and had I arrived an hour earlier, the whole family would have been killed at lunch. Friends and relations were deeply impressed by what appeared to have been a providential escape for all of us. Norah and Phyllis, who had been at home when the rocket fell, were both seriously injured. Two or three people in the house opposite were killed.

That afternoon and the following day Father and I salvaged whatever we could from the ruins. A few pieces of furniture and one or two carpets were still usable and the contents of drawers and cupboards largely intact. Though it was dangerous to do so, I insisted on climbing up the remaining stairs to see what had happened to my books. Out of a thousand, about four hundred were either destroyed or very badly damaged. The undamaged ones, which fortunately included most of the more valuable volumes, I removed and stacked on the lawn with the rest of the salvage. The floor of my room then collapsed.

Father having managed to borrow a truck, we removed the remnants of our home to Ewell, it having been understood between Uncle Charles and Father since the beginning of the war that the house of each would be at the disposal of the other in case of need. After returning to camp on Sunday night, I saw the CO on Monday morning and was granted a week's compassionate leave. From Leatherhead I went straight to Joan's camp, which was in a nearby town. She, too, was granted compassionate leave and the pair of us, now both in khaki, travelled up to Ewell. Somehow we felt very young and yet terribly old. Joan, who had taken the news in a calm, matter-of-fact way, now told me about her work. Though barely seventeen, she regularly took a two-ton lorry from the south coast all the way up to Scotland, driving at night, in convoy, and without lights. Father was, of course, very glad to see her, and the three of us spent the week at Ewell together quite happily. Uncle Charles's firm having again evacuated its staff, this time to Somerset, we had the house to ourselves.

Not long after my return to camp rumours began to circulate about the Unit having been posted abroad. The married men fervently hoped they were unfounded; but in Ernie and me and the rest of the youngsters vague nomadic longings stirred. Though for security reasons our destination was not revealed, the rumours were at first tacitly then expressly confirmed, until the whole camp was restless, excited, and there was no talk save of our impending departure. Tom, who was on confidential terms with one of the officers, told Ernie and me that our destination was definitely India. But with such a buzz of speculation around us, some saying it would be Gibraltar, some Singapore, and some even America, it was difficult to feel sure. Besides, that I should be going to India, the land in which the Buddha had lived and taught, seemed too good to be true. For the first, though by no means the last, time in my life, did I have an obscure sense of some mysterious Destiny shaping my ends. I had thought the army would cut me off from Buddhism. What if it should now prove the means appointed to bring me closer to it than I had dreamed would be possible?

At the beginning of August we were given a week's embarkation leave. Much of this time I spent arranging what was left of my library and tying my manuscript books in bundles. Two or three rare volumes, as well as the thick black notebook containing my most recent poems, I left with Clare. One or two days were spent with Nana in Somerset, where she was staying, not very happily, in the same village as Uncle Charles and Auntie Kath. When I said goodbye she clung to me tearfully as if she would never let me go. Both knew we would never meet again. Back in London, I took Sonia to see *Swan Lake*, dined out once or twice with Mother, and spent a few evenings at the local public house with Father. The final leave-takings were restrained and casual.

Three or four days later we entrained for the north. Most of the journey I spent writing poetry. But the bleak northern landscape, with its barren fields and squat stone hedges, fascinated me, and every now and then I lifted my eyes from the notebook and gazed out of the window. In the late afternoon on the second day the train stopped at the foot of a huge rock which, rising sheer for several hundred feet, tapered into the walls, battlements, and turrets of an ancient castle. Two or three hours later, rifles in hand, packs on our backs, and kitbags balanced on one shoulder, we stood on the quayside of the Glasgow docks waiting to file up the gangway into the bowels of the enormous grey troopship.

Two days later, as the convoy passed the northern coast of Scotland and swung out into the Atlantic, I celebrated my nineteenth birthday. England had been left behind, perhaps for ever. But where were we going? Five days later, in the middle of the Atlantic, half way to America, we still did not know the answer.

10. Passage to India

'D' deck, somewhere on which the Unit was quartered, was the fourth deck down. Ernie and I were crowded together with scores of other sweating naked bodies under the harsh glare of electric lights while around us the whole ship quivered and shook with the constant heavy pounding of the engines. Practically the entire space from hatch cover to bulkhead was occupied by long clamped-down tables where we ate during the day and on which some of us slept at night. Kitbags were stacked in corners and packs and water-bottles stowed away between the girders and the deckhead. Though stifled by the heat, most of us caught colds through our habit of sleeping as close as possible to the blowers. Prickly heat was made worse by our having to wash and bathe in warm sticky sea-water using gritty yellow sea-soap that refused to lather. Like the rest of the troops Ernie and I spent most of our time on the passenger and boat decks, elbowing our way aft through the slowly milling khaki mass. At night, stupefied rather than asleep, we lay on tables or benches or the deck, or hung side by side from the deckhead in hammocks. Loud snores and heavy breathing filled the darkness, in which glowed two or three small red lights. Dreaming feverish dreams, we could feel ourselves being still shaken by the mighty pulsations of the engines. In the morning, tired and sticky, we got up with relief and went for a latherless wash and shave in sea-water.

Not knowing when I would again see a library or book-shop, I had squeezed into my kitbag *The Light of Asia*, *Selections from Hegel*, *The Penguin Book of English Verse*, and a few other pocket volumes selected chiefly on account of their convenient size. The unit had won exemption from ship's duties on the grounds that it had work to do in the Set Room that had been rigged up in the monkey island; but atmospheric disturbances and the ship's dynamo made reception impossible. Since the only remaining call on our time was the ten o'clock lifeboat drill, I was therefore free to spend most of the day reading. Probably because of the conditions under which we were living, I read such poems as 'Heaven-Haven', 'The Haystack in the Floods', and 'Cynara' with a strangely troubled intensity of emotion. Every day I composed in my head and then wrote down two or three short poems. These eventually formed a sort of verse diary of my impressions of the voyage.

One morning we awoke to find the ship in blue waters. The convoy had altered course two or three days earlier, and we had passed Gibraltar in the night. From then onwards my poems were usually descriptive of the scenes we passed. Alexandria, a distant streak of gleaming white-ness between sea and sky, led to a poem on Alexander the Great, the desert to one beginning, 'The first camel I saw was a white one', and so on. At Port Said, which we reached at nightfall, everyone crowded excitedly to the rail to see what was, after five years of blackout, the marvel-lous sight of buildings outlined with thousands of yellow lights. Red and blue neon signs flared with unearthly splendour against the sky, the biggest and brightest of them an advertisement for Dewar's Whisky, seeming for once like the dazzling epiphany of another world. Most beautiful of all, the lights nearest the quayside picked out in the black depths of the dock waters inverted palaces of rippling gold.

As slowly we squeezed our way down through the Suez Canal, the banks seeming in places hardly wider than the ship itself, I never tired of watching the great foam-serpent at the water's edge as it raced abreast of the ship with an eager undulating movement. Sometimes I stared so long and hard that I could scarcely believe it was not a real live dragon keeping me friendly company like a faithful dog, instead of just the bow wash striking against the side of the canal.

At Suez we were allowed ashore. Though I had not been seasick the earth felt strangely firm underfoot. After a visit to the local restaurant, a low wooden shack where we ate eggs and bacon with an unusual amount of elbow room, Ernie and I spent half an hour exploring the dock area before finally climbing back on board. Aden, which we saw at twilight, was an enormous ash-heap at the foot of which ant-like figures crawled about among the cinders. But this dismal sight once left behind, day after day there was only the blue-black wrinkled expanse of the Indian Ocean, where porpoises played astern and flying-fish skimmed like silver arrows over the waves and where, at night, the phosphorescent wake streamed out through the darkness behind us a pale and ghostly green.

What would India be like? Long before the horizon thickened into land I started asking myself this question. The *Children's Encyclopaedia* had left vague memories of marble palaces and bewhiskered Rajput princes. Missionaries on furlough, appealing for our coppers at Sunday School, had given impressions of a land of mud huts where they lived in constant fear of martyrdom at the hands of fanatical grass-skirted savages. Uncle Dick had spoken of rickshaws. Regular Army NCOs who had been stationed in India described it as the hottest, poorest, filthiest country on earth and the 'wogs' as the very dregs of humanity. It seemed difficult to fit the Buddha and his teaching into any of these backgrounds.

What gradually hove in sight through the drizzle of a late September morning (we were in the midst of a different set of seasons and had run into the tail end of the monsoon) was a stretch of Bombay dockside under a low grey sky. As we edged nearer through the dingy water, more like ochre-coloured liquid mud than anything else, oblong boxes grew by degrees into huge warehouses of corrugated iron. Here and there a crane hung idle against the sky. The odd knots of blue-clad figures on the quay did not seem to be doing anything in particular. There was no noise. The whole place seemed half dead. Only the kites, rising and falling in endless spirals overhead, seemed more or less alive.

From the back of the lorry that took us to the station we had a glimpse of tree-lined streets, bullock-carts, and thin dark figures in flapping off-white garments. On the journey to Delhi, which we made in bogies with hard wooden benches instead of upholstered seats, ghastly poverty whined around us whenever the train stopped. Emaciated women in filthy rags pushed rusty tins through the windows and pleaded with gentle insistence for alms. Spindly-limbed children with enormous protruding bellies clamoured for coins and scraps of food. Gauntly naked men, in an attempt to excite pity, pointed to deformed or missing limbs. Half the beggars seemed blind or halt or maimed. One, quite naked, moved from carriage to carriage exhibiting testicles swollen to the size of footballs. Horrified at the sight of poverty such as they had never imagined could exist, most of the BORs handed out small coins and food at every station. The Indian troops a little farther down the train, doubtless more accustomed to such sights, leaned grinning from the windows and gave nothing. Even more dreadful than the poverty was the apathy, the patient hopeless resignation, apparent on the faces of the beggars. Their shoulders were bowed and their heads bent in uncomplaining acceptance of their lot. It was God's will, they seemed to be saying, God's will be done!

The camp outside Delhi consisted of a dozen buildings with thatched roofs and dazzlingly white walls surrounded by sand and scrub on which the sun blazed down from a sky more deeply and darkly blue than I had ever known. In between the barracks, shading them from the glare, could be seen the bushy, light-green foliage of the margosa trees. Grey-brown squirrels with three white stripes down their backs raced chattering up and down the smooth trunks, sometimes pausing in between flicks of their bushy tails to cling motionless for an instant with bright beady eyes. Crows in pearl-grey cravats perched on the roofs, while overhead hovered more kites which, effortlessly rising and falling hour after hour, described great sweeps whenever their outstretched wings were caught by an air-current.

Owing largely to the heat, at that time of year so intense that the landscape quivered, army life in India had developed a pattern of its own. There were no general duties. In our case there were no parades or military duties of any kind either. All the menial work of the camp was done by Indian bearers. Operators were on duty only half the day, one week mornings one week afternoons, the rest of the time being their own. In the Set Room, where most of us wore nothing but shorts and canvas shoes, a quiet drowsy atmosphere prevailed. Only an occasional muffled shriek from somebody's headphones disturbed the stillness. Very little work was done. Most of my time was spent scribbling poems on scraps of paper. Sometimes I watched the bulgy-eyed, semi-transparent orange geckoes suckered onto the wall. Every now and then one of them would make a loud clicking sound. Once a praying mantis, vivid green and with a face like the head of a safety pin, whirred onto my set and perched there motionless. At ten in the morning and four in the afternoon would come the licensed cake-wallah. A good part of our pay was spent each week buying little sweet cakes covered with multi-coloured icing, three or four of which we always took with our mugs of dark, bitter-tasting tea.

In the lofty-ceilinged barrack room it was comparatively cool. Seven or eight charpoys, wooden bedsteads with a network of coarse fibre rope instead of springs, stood with their heads against the wall. Six-foot bamboos, lashed to the legs of the charpoys, supported the mosquito-nets, whereunder much of our time was spent in the traditional recumbent posture of the British soldier in India. A door, through which I could see the scrubby yellow landscape and intensely blue sky, opened on to a veranda which ran the whole length of the building. Here the dhobi-wallah, the cake-wallah, and our own bearers, in green, brown, and blue lungis, would squat on their heels quietly chatting, occasionally glancing up through the doorway with bright, furtive eyes. For the first week Myers's trilogy *The Far and the Near*, which I had borrowed from a room-mate, absorbed my whole attention. With its background of sophisticated court life at Agra and Delhi during the reign of Akbar it was a fitting introduction to the glory and grandeur that had been Moghul India.

Half a mile from camp was a small bazaar. Here, in a tiny restaurant exhibiting the blue-wheeled 'in bounds' sign, Ernie and I sometimes sat among the cracked wall mirrors at a marble-topped table, drinking iced Vimto through double straws. When he came to take our order, the proprietor cheerfully wiped the table with a filthy rag. In a shop which sold magazines, stationery, and picture postcards I discovered a couple of shelves of books. As is usual in Indian bookstalls, pornography and religion rubbed shoulders. An English translation of the *Bhagavad Gita*, which I purchased for a few annas, was keeping company with *The Adventures of Erotic Edna* and *Hindu Art of Love (Illustrated)*. Later, especially in south India, I often found articles on God-Realization and frankly worded advertisements for aphrodisiacs printed side by side in the same magazine. India believed, apparently, in impartial catering for all tastes.

When I had been on morning duty I usually spent the afternoon and evening in the city. Sometimes I walked several miles along the Agra–Delhi road before getting a lift from a passing army truck. The flat, rocky landscape, barren save for the tender green of stunted thorn-trees, had a delicate austere beauty which touched me more deeply than anything I had seen in England. Lush meadows and leafy woods seemed, in fact, rather vulgar in comparison. It was an aloof, aristocratic landscape which somehow suggested centuries of culture and refinement. Usually neither a house nor a human being was in sight. Once or twice I saw a figure that might have come from the Old Testament standing motionless on a rock while little white goats with black and brown markings and blunt faces streamed among the nullahs nibbling at tufts of wiry grass.

The contrast between the red sandstone walls of the Lal Khila, or Red Fort, massive enough to enclose a town, and the row of white marble palace buildings that overlooked the River Jumna from the rear battlements, struck me as tremendously effective. Is not this wedding of strength and grace, of the stupendous and the delicate, one of the greatest charms of Moghul architecture? While I would not attempt to erect a personal preference into an objective aesthetic judgement, its austerely beautiful mosques and tombs, its palaces and forts, have often satisfied me more deeply than the prodigal richness, the unrestrained exuberance, of their Hindu counterparts. Indeed, they have often satisfied me more deeply than their Indian Buddhist counterparts. As I stood in the multi-columned Diwan-i-Khas, or Hall of Private Audience, where at the feet of emperors a shallow stream had once flowed over a gem-studded silver bed—flowed the length of the building and out under the pierced marble screens into the private apartments—I felt the truth of the Persian couplet inscribed in flawlessly beautiful calligraphy above the windows overlooking the treetops and the slow, sad river: 'If there is Paradise upon the face of the earth, it is here, it is here, it is here'.

In Sher Shah's mosque, which I also visited, red sandstone and white marble had united to create a building with all the majesty of a fort and the beauty of a palace. The contrast between the austere squareness of the façade and the soaring curves of the lofty lancet arches by which it was pierced thrilled me with exquisitely painful pleasure.

From the grass-grown ruins of the Purana Khila, the Old Fort, not far away, I peered down over ancient weathered battlements at a sea of darkly massed treetops. The sun was setting and the dusky tender greens and burnt reds of the landscape now glowed softly in a flood of pale amber light. Suddenly a flock of parakeets flew across the treetops, tiny spurts of greenness against the dark tangle of the vegetation below.

Occasionally, restless for I knew not what, I spent the afternoon wandering round the arcades of Connaught Circus. Hawkers squatting on the pavements offered cheap flashy curios at exorbitant prices. In the windows of the ivory marts elaborately carved boxes and statuettes were displayed against Persian carpets. Once, crossing the road to the next block, I saw in the distance the three onion domes of the Jamma Masjid, or Friday Mosque. Before long I found a bookshop. Rimbaud's poems, one of the first books I bought, delighted me even more than Baudelaire's, which I had read shortly before leaving England. Perhaps this was because of their tropical brilliance of colouring, which seemed in perfect keeping with my present surroundings. Certainly 'I have seen the dawn arisen like a flock of doves' was truer of India than of England. The collected poems of Sarojini Naidu, *The Nightingales of India*, though lushly rhetorical, interested me so much that I wrote on them an article, published in *The Poetry Review*, entitled 'Krishna's Flute'. No doubt it was not their poetry which appealed to me so much as their vivid pictures of India. For all its poverty and filth the great subcontinent had already begun to cast upon me, as upon so many other Englishmen, the subtle spell of its unrivalled fascination.

At night, aching from the peregrinations of the day and feeling somehow frustrated, I ate ices in a milk bar or hung around the corner waiting for the driver of the 'liberty wagon' which would take us back to camp. As we rushed through the blackness of the night along the deserted highway, with the wind fresh in our faces and the sky thick with brilliant stars, it seemed, after the heat and dazzle of the day, that life had no purer enjoyment to offer. Alighting at the top of the road, I walked back to the barracks, past the old gymnasium on the left and the distant lights of the KOYLI camp over to the right, while millions of cicadas throbbed and shrilled and sang from the grass and jackals howled and barked in the far distance.

Among the books I had bought in Connaught Circus was an English translation of the *Aporakshanubhuti*, a treatise by the great non-dualist Hindu philosopher, Shankara. In it was described a method of meditation by dissociating oneself successively from the body, the mind, and the empirical ego. At night, seated cross-legged inside the mosquito curtain while the other inmates of the room slept, I practised according to the instructions given in the book. 'I am not the body, I am not the mind,' I reflected, 'I am the non-dual Reality, the Brahman; I am the Absolute Existence-Knowledge-Bliss.' As I practised, body-consciousness faded away and my whole being was permeated by a great peaceful joy. One night there appeared before me, as it were suspended in mid-air, the head of an old man. He had a grey stubble on scalp and chin and his yellowish face was deeply lined and wrinkled as though by the sins and vices of a lifetime. 'You're wasting your time,' he exclaimed, with a dreadful sneer. 'There's nothing in the universe but matter. Nothing but matter.'

'There is something higher than matter,' I promptly retorted, 'I know it, because I am experiencing it now.' Whereupon the apparition vanished. Years later, during my second visit to Nepal, I saw the same Mara, as it must have been. I recognized him at once, and he no doubt recognized me.

According to the guide book, the Lakshmi-Narayan Temple was the most important Hindu shrine in New Delhi. But the driver of the *ekka*, or horse-drawn carriage I hired to take me there, did not seem to know where it was. Perhaps he knew it by its popular name, Birla Mandir, after the multi-millionaire who had donated the funds for its construction. Perhaps he wanted to take me by a circuitous route and charge for a whole afternoon's hire—a common trick with *ekka*-drivers. Whichever it was, after jolting along for two hours in the little two-wheeled trap, I found myself not in the temple in New Delhi but in a *dharmashala*, or pilgrims' rest house, in Old Delhi, about six miles away. Here I was finally rescued by a friendly, English-educated young Indian, the first to whom I had spoken, who not only accompanied me all the way back to New Delhi but took the trouble of showing me round the temple precincts.

The Lakshmi-Narayan Temple, an imposing building in a sort of neo-Hindu style of architecture, stood in spacious grounds where pink cement paths ran between small artificial ponds. Inside there was a great deal of marble of various colours, and a bewilderingly large number of gods and goddesses, one painted bright blue and another with an elephant's head. Stranger still, there was a shrine dedicated to Guru Nanak, the founder of Sikhism, whom I had always thought was not a Hindu but a Sikh. Behind the temple extended a garden where noisy crowds sauntered among pink cement elephants and looked into artificial caves, the mouths of which were painted to resemble the open jaws of mythological beasts. The bright pinks and greens and yellows of the coloured cement reminded me of the little iced cakes we brought from the cake-wallah.

Retracing our steps, my Indian friend and I passed between two more pink elephants into a side garden. Fronting the road from behind its own iron gate stood a temple of modest dimensions and distinctive architectural style. Removing my shoes, I ascended the two or three white marble steps and for the first time in my life found myself in a Buddhist temple. Facing me from the far end was a life-size image of the Buddha. Before it on the white marble altar candles burned among offerings of flowers. Incense hung in the air. The stillness was intense. After buying a copy of the *Dhammapada* and other literature at the stall inside the entrance I explored the rest of the enclosure. On a patch of lawn outside the tiny bungalow next door two or three bright yellow robes had been spread to dry in the sun. In the hope of being able to meet a Buddhist monk I tried the door. It was locked from within. The windows were shuttered. There seemed to be no sign of life in the place at all.

Appendix

In his Introduction, Sangharakshita mentioned the thorough revisions he made to Chapter One in 1973. While resulting in a more consistent piece of work, these revisions necessarily involved a considerable sacrifice of detail. The full text of the original, unrevised first Chapter is therefore reproduced here:

1. Giants And Dragons

Apart from my refusal to cry when born, the strangest circumstance of my most recent appearance in this world on 26 August 1925 is that it took place in a nursing home in south-west London only a few hundred yards from the spot where, two years earlier, had died Allen Bennett, otherwise Ananda Maitreya, the first Englishman to take the yellow robe in the East and return to teach the Dharma in his native land.

My parents at that time occupied the upper part of a house in Tooting which belonged to my grandmother. Brick-walled and slate-roofed, with green privet hedge, a pair of highly polished front doors—one for the upstairs the other for the downstairs flat—and lace-curtained windows, it was one of the hundreds of thousands which, standing back to back in interminable rows, help to make up that vast maze of mutually intersecting streets which is suburban London.

What I take to be my earliest memory, however, finds me not outside but inside the house. Lying at night in the great double bed in my parents' room, which was at the front of the house, I used to stare up at the foliated ceiling piece, the size and shape of a cartwheel, from the centre of which hung the light. As motors passed up and down the main road which was at the bottom of our street, their headlights, reflected on to the ceiling, swung slowly round the centre-piece like great bright spokes around a shadowy hub. If the motors were going south, towards the coast, the spokes swung clockwise; if north, to the city's heart, in the opposite direction. With the clanging of distant tram-bells and the low roar and rumble of the other traffic in my ears I used to lie in the darkness and watch the spokes turning now this way, now that, and now both ways simultaneously as two motors crossed each other, until lulled to sleep. In later years, when I slept in my own bedroom, I used to experience the sensation of being whirled round and round into a great golden light which gradually engulfed me and I knew no more. Whether the later experience, which continued until I was five or six, was connected with the earlier, I do not know; but for quite a long time after it had ceased I took it for granted that everyone fell asleep in the same manner.

As I grew older I naturally became dissatisfied with passive contemplation: 'Mother, can I go out and play?' was my constant cry. The natural playground of the London child is, of course, the street, but there I was not allowed to play until after I had started school. In the meantime, therefore, I played on the black and white tiles of the porch and behind the dusty privet with my sister, fifteen months younger than myself, and a girl of my own age who lived down the road at No. 1 (our house was No. 23) a game of our own invention called Old Mother

Witchie. Sometimes we played so noisily that 'the lady downstairs', a kindly old soul who used to send us up jelly and trifle in tumblers, had to tap gently on the window of her front room to silence us, for although we did not know it her husband, who died not long afterwards, was seriously ill.

When it rained, or when I was not allowed to play 'out in the front', my refrain was 'Mother, can Frances come in to play?' Usually she could. Our favourite game was 'dressing up', for which we ransacked the house for old lace curtains. As a special treat we were sometimes allowed to borrow the embroidered veil in which my father and I had been christened, and then great was our joy, for instead of playing Fathers and Mothers, as we usually did, we could play at weddings. I was the bridegroom, Frances the bride, and my sister sometimes the bridesmaid and sometimes the officiating clergyman. This love of dressing up persisted much longer in my case than it did in that of the girls, and even at the age of eight I could spend hours in front of the long mirror in my parents' bedroom experimenting with different styles of dress. Jersey and knickerbockers were not my real costume, I felt sure, and almost desperately I swathed and draped myself in lengths of material, searching in vain for my true vesture. The only times I felt satisfied was when, with the help of a Red Ensign, I achieved, more by accident than design, a toga-like effect which, though not exactly right, was to some extent what I desired. Then, gravely holding my grandfather's silver-mounted amber cane, I would stand gazing at my reflection which solemn pleasure for several minutes.

On days when I had no playmate I used to crawl beneath the dining room table and amuse myself by scrawling on its underside with coloured crayons. How often my mother left me alone in the house while she went out shopping I no longer recollect, but I remember her solemn adjuration not to open the door if anyone knocked and the precipitation with which, in anticipation of some terrible visitor, I used to take refuge beneath this table as soon as she had gone. On her return she would usually find me still crouching there, my heart pounding with terror. Experiences of this sort gave rise to frequent nightmares, frightful variations on the theme of waking dread. In one, great heavy footsteps would drag slowly up the stairs, along the passage, and into the room, until from my refuge I could see, as it were, the feet of the unknown evil and woke screaming. In another the tramp of an approaching army would come closer and closer upon me, full of infinite menace and horror, while I would be rooted with terror to the spot, unable to move. For several years I was afraid to go to bed, and still more afraid to sleep. Memory of the nightmares made me yet more terrified if my mother left me alone during the day, and perhaps it was not altogether without dread that I played underneath the table while she was at home.

A much less unpleasant memory of this friendly piece of furniture is of being called out from underneath it one morning to be told that Uncle Tom, my godfather, was dead. This red-faced, white-haired old gentleman, with a rough and hearty manner and a savage temper, used to call me to his knee on my birthday and other state occasions and make me hold out my hand while he counted into it as many half-crowns as he was in a humour to give. He lived across the road with his niece, a thin, meek, rheumy-eyed woman whom he treated with great harshness, believing that she cared for him only in the hope of being left his money. On the wall of the room where I sometimes visited him hung a glass case containing a stuffed red fox with a pigeon in its mouth. From the day I saw it I coveted this wonder, and I believe I had been promised it. As soon as I heard the news of my godfather's death I therefore eagerly inquired: 'Now shall I get the fox?' Though this brutally direct question for the moment horrified my parents, they were too sensible to take serious exception to a child's lack of feeling. Besides, my enquiry was not unjustified. From conversations which I had overheard I knew that Uncle Tom, who was not related to us in any way, had several times proposed marriage to my grandmother, promising, as an additional inducement, to make me his heir if she would accept him. My grandmother, who had already buried two husbands, told him plainly that she had no desire to bury a third and that it was his duty to leave his money to his niece; but as she and Uncle Tom were still friends and often went out on excursions together, it was generally assumed that he had probably remembered me in his will. In the end the wilful old man left all his money to very distant relations and neither the niece nor I got anything—not even the fox!

My grandmother, who occupied a place in my affections hardly second to that of my parents, lived at Southfields in another house which belonged to her. Among my earliest recollections is that of my father taking us to see her on fine Sunday mornings in the perambulator, with its cream-coloured awning. When I was old enough to walk we went by tram to Earlsfield station, whence we strolled through the side streets to the quiet road, more select than ours, where she lived. As soon as my father swung open the iron front gate, I used to run up the path and rattle the shining brass letterbox until either Nana, as I always called her, or Auntie Noni, came to let us in, all the time peering eagerly through the stained glass panels of the big dark green front door. The hall never failed to interest me, and never did I pass through it without pausing to look up at the Nepalese kukris and Chinese swords and chopstick-sets with which the walls were decorated, and rarely could I refrain from ringing the Tibetan ritual handbell which stood in a corner behind the door.

But what drew my attention most of all was the big Chinese picture on the left-hand wall. This my father had lifted me up to see ever since I was a baby and it was thus among the most familiar objects of my childhood. Almost square in shape, it depicted an august and mysterious personage seated cross-legged on a kind of throne. He was arrayed in loosely flowing robes and behind his head was a nimbus. His features, which were markedly oriental, with slant eyes that gazed far into the distance, were expressive of a remarkable combination of benignity and power. This enigmatic being was surrounded by half a dozen figures, some making offerings, others playing on musical instruments, and all not more than a tenth of the size of their master, whom, for this reason, I called the Giant.

Running into the sitting-room, at the far end of which glass doors opened into the conservatory where one of the cacti, so my father assured me, bore a single red rose-like flower every seven years, I found objects to gaze at and even handle which were hardly less wonderful than those in the hall. The Chinese cloisonné vases, of which there were several pairs, were as fine as any which, in later years, I saw in Tibetan temples and at the houses of Chinese friends, and the shape of some has been in my experience unique. One great flagon-shaped pair with gold dragon handles depicted houses, gardens, and human figures. Even now, at a distance of thirty years, I can see a favourite figure in blue gown and black cap, standing pensively among the toy hills. Round each of the other vases, all of which were a deep rich blue, coiled a five-clawed imperial dragon, with liver-coloured body, yellow head, red horns, black eyes, purple mane, and scales picked out in gold. Each dragon had its jewel and spat flame as if in its defence. Of these mysterious beasts it never occurred to me to feel afraid, and certainly they were never for me, as they are for the Christian tradition, symbolical of evil, so that it was without astonishment that I learned, in later life, that to the Chinese the dragon had been for thousands of years the symbol of the Yang, the bright, masculine, creative principle of the universe, even as the phoenix, with which I was unacquainted, was the symbol of the Yin, the dark, feminine, destructive principle. Was it because of this early acquaintance with dragons that I have never been afraid of snakes, but even as a child longed to stroke their smooth silken bodies—neither cold nor clammy, as those who ignorantly shrink from them imagine—and have them coiling about my hands—that, in fact, I had a strange love for all reptiles, even the common toad? Children are animists to whom nothing is dead, and to me my dragons were not pictures on vases but friendly shapes with whom I played whenever I went to my grandmother's house, and with whom, perhaps, in some luminous underground chamber of my mind, I am playing still.

On the white marble mantelpiece, between the Westminster chime clock and the flagon-shaped vase on the right, was a small sedent bronze image which, when able to talk, I called the Empress Dowager. When I shook it, it rattled. Now I know that the figure my baby fingers clutched, the features of which I can remember as well as those of any human face, represented not the last imperial ruler of China but the 'Goddess of Mercy', Kwan Yin, the feminized Chinese version of the Bodhisattva Avalokiteshvara, one of the most popular figures of the Indian Buddhist pantheon. The rattling noise must have been produced not, as I then supposed, by a stone, but by one of those holy relics which the Buddhists of China, like those of Tibet, frequently seal in images. Strange it is that in those days I should have met as an image the great spiritual being who, in later years, became to me a living presence!

But in what mysterious way did the Buddha, the dragons, and the Chinese goddess come to make their appearance in that English household? How was it that a boy of three or four could be in a position to make so free with the name of the last of the Empresses? At this point an English family chronicle and Chinese history intersect.

In Nana's dining-room there hung, on opposite walls, the portraits of two men, one in naval the other in military uniform. The man in the first, which was considerably larger, wore a walrus moustache and must have been about thirty. The man in the second picture, which was slightly yellowed, had a small trim moustache and seemed to be in his early twenties. It puzzled me very much in that time to be told that both men were my grandfather for, as from Uncle Tom's courtship it has already transpired, my grandmother had been twice married and moreover had had four children, first my father, then my Auntie Noni and then, after an interval of several years, another boy, my Uncle Charles, who, like Auntie Noni, still lived with her, and a girl, Dorothy, who had died young and whom I never saw.

It was her second husband, about whom I gathered little more than is recorded here, who was responsible for the introduction into the house of the exotic objects described. Of partly Portuguese descent, he had travelled widely, at one time serving in the Merchant Navy. At the time of the Boxer Rebellion he was working for the Imperial Government of China as a commissioner of railways and, having a mania for curios, took advantage of the opportunity afforded by the sack of the Summer Palace at Pekin to add to his collection. Though the greater part was dispersed after his death, as my grandmother disliked having to dust grass skirts and polish spears every day, and my father objected to living with the cases of live shells on the wall, much remained, most of which passed to Uncle Charles. Among the things which she had kept were three of the Empress's bedspreads of yellow silk worked with gold dragons, tiny butterfly shoes, and a number of embroidered silk robes. These and the cloisonné vases had come from the Summer Palace; the picture in the hall, the figure of Kwan Yin, and the bell behind the front door, from the Lama Temple.

Grandfather was also a photographer, it seems, for there was an album of photographs taken at the time of the rebellion. Kneeling on the ground with their hands pinioned behind their backs were rows of naked rebels, some with their severed heads already at the executioner's feet. My sister and I spent many happy hours looking at these pictures, which were kept at the bottom of a curio cabinet, until one day Nana realized that they were not the most suitable thing for children to see. Years later I found them with Uncle Charles who, being sadistic and acquisitive, had eventually laid claim to them.

About Nana's first husband, albeit he was my own grandfather, I knew hardly as much as I did about her second, partly, perhaps, because he had died so young that my father had no recollection of him to share with me. He came, I gathered, of a good Suffolk family and was the youngest of eight brothers. How he met Nana, the daughter of a Norfolk farmer, I do not know. But perhaps he married her against the wishes of his parents, for never, to my knowledge, did my father have any dealings with his paternal aunts and uncles. Only years later and when, just before I left England, they started dying off at a ripe old age—leaving what was left of the money they had inherited from their mother, who had been an heiress, to be shared among my father, Auntie Noni, and a cousin—did I even hear their names.

After their marriage Nana and grandfather lived at Woolwich where, in 1899, my father was born. Grandfather was then working at the War Office, where he made out the officers' commissions which went to the Queen for signature. Years later, in the Natural History Museum at South Kensington, Father showed me the famous War Office cat, as large as a bull terrier, on which as a very small boy he had been given rides. Grandfather also handled foreign despatches, for when, shortly after being himself commissioned, he died suddenly after a short illness, the family physician attributed his death to germs which had been transmitted through these papers. Nana believed that he died of pneumonia.

Be the cause what it may, his death left Nana to support two small children, one of them still a baby. But being a woman of very decided character she met the situation courageously and resolved to work. From odd reminiscences of hers in later years I gathered that at different times she had been a cleaner, a parlour-maid, and a housekeeper. Probably it was for the sake of security that, after five or six years of this hard life, she married for the second time and thus came to live at Tooting. She once told my mother, whom she loved as her own daughter, that she remembered her first husband much better than her second, from which the romantically inclined may conclude that she had loved him much more. To my mother's question, 'Doesn't your first marriage seem rather vague to you after so many years?', she at once replied with a joyous expression: 'Oh no, it's all as fresh as if it had happened yesterday!' Whatever the difference in her feelings about her two husbands might or might not have been, their memories were honoured equally, and thus it was throughout my childhood and adolescence my two grandfathers continued to regard each other across the dining-room table.

Between my father and his sister, who was also my

godmother, existed a very deep and strong affection; in fact they were in many ways much alike. Besides inheriting Nana's heavy eyebrows, blue-grey eyes, and aquiline nose, they were both, like her, outspoken in opinion and firm in adherence to principle. But whereas Auntie Noni was exceptionally self-possessed and could make the deadliest remarks with the utmost coolness—especially to my mother, who would sometimes be reduced either to helpless fury or to tears, both of which Auntie Noni regarded with equanimity—my father was, or at least in his youth had been, as I knew from his own confession, hot-tempered in the extreme and almost morbidly quick to take offence. But being of a generous and forgiving nature his anger never lasted long, and by the time I was born his temper was more or less under control, only an occasional flash showing that there was still lightning in the cloud. He was in fact on the whole an unusually good man and apart from the Indian and Tibetan saints I afterwards met I never knew anyone to whom unselfishness was so natural, or who so cheerfully put the pleasure and happiness of others before his own.

Auntie Noni hero-worshipped him, which was natural, but unfortunately could not refrain from singing his praises to my mother who, however much she loved my father, could hardly have enjoyed being told, as she frequently was, what a good man she had married and how lucky she was to have married him. This last remark was always conveyed in a tone which suggested that having such a man for a husband was a miracle for which my mother should go down on her unworthy knees and render thanks to heaven.

Auntie Noni was herself unmarried. Her fiancé, my father's best friend, had been killed in the Great War, and so much did she cherish his memory that she preferred to remain single.

Unlike Mother, both my father and Auntie Noni had a very lively sense of humour and were excellent raconteurs. If at home my cry was: 'Mother, can I go out and play?', at Nana's it was: 'Auntie, tell me a story'. Auntie Noni's stories were all about a little boy called Dicky Doughnut and Mrs Jellybottom, his aunt, and always ended disastrously for poor Mrs Jellybottom who, by the mischievous contrivance of Dicky, would be unexpectedly deluged with blancmange, or precipitated head first into a bowl of cream. At the climax of these stories I would clap my hands in excitement and shriek with delight. My father, a glass of wine in his hand and a sausage roll before him (the customary last refection) would laugh good-naturedly and Nana would wipe the tears from her eyes, for they all enjoyed these stories. When I was an adolescent Uncle Charles used to tease me by telling his small son to call me Dicky Doughnut, it having been generally understood that the hero of Auntie Noni's stories was in fact none other than myself.

My father's stories, which he told me when I had been put to bed, were of two kinds, true and imaginary. Most of the true stories were about his own life, especially his schooldays and experiences as a soldier in the trenches during the Great War. The imaginary stories, in the telling of which he must have drawn upon great sources of inventiveness, as he had to tell me a new one every night for a number of years, were all tales of adventure. In fact his secret ambition, which circumstances did not permit to be fulfilled, was to be a writer, and I attribute his subsequent connivance at my own literary aspirations to the feeling that his youthful ambition might one day be realized in the person of his son.

The then vivid and exciting stories are now only a very vague and general impression from which his accounts of how he gave a false age to be able to enlist, lived under shellfire, saw comrades blown to bits, and was himself wounded and woke up in a hospital tent without the use of the right hand, which was permanently disabled, project like hilltops above the surrounding mists. Little did he think, as he told me these stories, that when I was his age I would have war experiences of my own to relate!

In the Church Lane Hospital, Upper Tooting, where he convalesced, he met my mother, who worked there as a member of the Voluntary Aid Detachment. One of his more amusing stories was about her helping him clamber over the hospital wall at night when he had stayed out after hours. They were married in 1919. My father was then nineteen, my mother perhaps twenty. I say 'perhaps' because Mother subsequently declared that she was younger than Father, a claim which he refuted by recalling how, in the early years of marriage, she tried to settle any difference of opinion between them by saying that she was a year older than he was and ought to know better. But as Father was always rather a wag I am not quite sure whether this story is to be classified as true or imaginary. After their marriage they lived for a short time at Merton Park, just over the border of Metropolitan London, removing thence to the house at Tooting when, on the death of her second husband, Nana shifted to Southfields.

The road in which the house was situated ran from east to west about half a mile. At the corner which our side of the street made with the main road stood the dairy, from which every afternoon at four o'clock the dog belonging to 'the lady downstairs' could be seen carrying home in his mouth his daily bar of Nestlé's chocolate. To this dairy my sister Joan and I were sometimes sent for butter or eggs and while waiting to be served we would feel the coldness of the marble counter with our foreheads and look wonderingly at the rows of stoppered glass jars filled with wafer biscuits wrapped in varicoloured silver paper.

When she was in a good mood the proprietress would give us each a pair of cardboard Oxo spectacles. Often, while there, we would turn round at the sound of the bell to see hobbling in the familiar figure of an incredibly ancient crone dressed from head to foot in rusty black with the yellowest parchment-like face I ever saw. But the most familiar thing about her was neither her face nor her clothes but her odour, which we could have recognized with our eyes shut and which was so bad that I can still smell it when I think of her. On the opposite corner stood a pet shop, in the window of which could be seen little day-old chicks and white rabbits, and, next door to the pet shop, a sweet shop of which Joan and I were regular patrons for many years, running there whenever we had a copper to spend.

Less than half way up the street on the other side of the road rose the grey stone and yellow brick mass of the school which my father had attended as a boy and to which at the age of four I, too, was sent. The building was by no means unfamiliar to me. Had I not seen its green cupolas against the sky and heard its bell ringing twice a day ever since I could remember? But so frightened was I on the day of my admission that at the first opportunity I ran home. This reluctance to study did not last long and four not unhappy years did I spend in the infants' department—the longest period of continuous schooling I was ever to receive.

From the confused whirl of impressions belonging to that time some stand out with special vividness: the beautiful swans which, when we were in the bottom class, we were taught to draw on the blackboards; the much-hated afternoon siesta on folding cots in the hall; the brass bell on the headmistress's desk; the cup of hot cocoa which, on a cold winter's day, my mother handed me through the iron railings at playtime—an act of indulgence for which she was duly rebuked; the paper lunch-bags pencilled with our names which were kept in the wastepaper basket until the morning break when the names were read out and the bags redistributed; dear old Mrs Davies' my teacher's flowered housecoat and the alarming manner in which her eyeballs bulged as she threaded a needle; the agony of not being allowed to go outside to the lavatory and the shame when bowels could no longer be controlled and when, after letting out a sudden howl in the middle of a lesson, I was led off home in tears; the day on which my mother, washing me for afternoon school, saw on my arm the red weal of the slapping I had received in the morning from a new teacher, and on going to complain to the headmistress, found her desk besieged by a score of indignant mothers with the same complaint; the tall flowers in the school garden which, since they were known to us as red hot pokers, I thought would burn me if I touched them; the breaking-up party with its buns and lemonade at which I appeared as a Red Indian and Joan as a fairy; the headmistress's shoes each with three straps and each strap fastened with a button; the kiss I exchanged under the desk with a little girl when I was in the top class; the potted aspidistras in the hall which the older pupils considered it a great distinction to be asked to water; the unutterable boredom of spelling and arithmetic lessons when it seemed the period would never end; the uproarious delight with which, the minute the 'going home' bell rang, we would tumble pell-mell out of the classroom, round the lobby for our hats and coats, and out of the gate home to tell our mothers what had happened during the day.

None of these seem to be of any special significance, but an autobiography, unlike a biography, is less a collection of facts than an evocation of memories, from the degree of whose distinctness the more delicately perceptive may gauge both the relative intensity of the experiences whose impressions they are and the nature and ultimate extent of the influence exerted by those experiences on the development of character and formation of opinion in the narrator. If this is disputed it will at least be conceded that, in weaving the fabric of autobiography the warp of significant incident can hardly be woven except upon the woof of its less interesting counterpart. In this field it is surely unreasonable to expect every common bush of anecdote to be afire with divine significance.

After tea on weekdays, all day on Saturday (though not usually on Sunday), as well as practically every day during the holidays, we were free to play in the street. Frances, Joan, and I always shared our games, for though we knew many other girls and boys, we formed a self-contained little confederacy and were happiest playing with one another. Frances, who was uncommonly quick and intelligent, often defeated me and I remember with what sorrow in my heart I once went to her house with a whole bagful of marbles to ransom a particularly large glass favourite she had won from me.

We never played all our games in one day. In fact as I look back it appears that our games had their cycles and that the investigating anthropologist would very likely find that conkers and marbles, tops and hopscotch, came and went in accordance with laws as immutable as those of economics. Conkers were available only in autumn. But there was no observable reason why, at one time, for weeks on end we should do nothing but lash tops, and at another devote ourselves exclusively to yo-yos, both of which could always be bought at the toyshop.

An anthropologist might also be able to tell me why, with the same infallibility of instinct with which a bird starts building its nest at the proper season, all the children of the district would begin making grottoes on or about a certain date in August, any attempt to set them up earlier or prolong their existence for more than three weeks being regarded as extremely reprehensible.

These grottoes, which were always built on the pavement against a wall, consisted of shells or small stones arranged in the form of a square, within which could be set flowers, small pieces of crockery, and any bright or curious object. After constructing the grottoes we had the right to sit by them and demand coppers from the passersby. Rarely were we disappointed. In the evening the grottoes were dismantled, being set up again next day from the same materials in another place. As we got older Frances, Joan, and I used to make our grottoes not only in our own street but in the neighbouring streets too, setting them up a yard or so apart against the same wall.

Another event which loomed large in our year was Derby Day, when throughout the afternoon and evening and until late at night a continuous stream of cars, buses, coaches, and horsedrawn carts and carriages, all packed with happy and excited racegoers, would be flowing along the main road between London and Epsom. Waving red, white, and blue streamers and holding to their mouths an instrument of wood and oiled paper which, when blown, would not only emit a raucous blare but, suddenly uncoiling to its full length, strike full in the face the unwary person at whom it was pointed, swarms of excited children would be standing on the kerb, their parents generally hovering behind to see that they did not fall under the wheels of the vehicles. When, races over and bets lost and won, the stream of traffic set more and more steadily in the homeward direction, our excitement reached its climax. Each brightly lit coach that swung slowly past us would be greeted by a shout of: 'Throw out your mouldies!' whereupon the beerily jovial occupants would respond by flinging into our midst a handful of coppers for which we scrambled and fought until the next coach came along. At intervals, with the crack of a whip and the jingle of be-ribboned harness, there would pass by, in all the glory of innumerable gleaming pearl buttons, a Pearly King and Queen. They were always stout, elderly, and smiling, and the Queen, who was generally stouter than the King and who smiled more broadly and laughed with greater hear-tiness, invariably wore a wide black hat with enormous ostrich plumes that nodded and danced at every step the pony took.

After putting Joan and me to bed my parents would go for a drink at the Trafalgar, a public house named in honour of the famous victory of good Lord Nelson who had lived at Merton, outside which, as outside every other public house in London that night, would be jammed a solid mass of people trying to elbow their way into the suffocating atmosphere of the bars.

Yet another annual event was Guy Fawkes Day. One year, when I was seven or eight, Mrs Davies wrote on the blackboard:

'Please to remember the Fifth of November,
Gunpowder, treason, and plot.'

Though another boy could read 'please', I was the only member of the class who could read 'remember' and 'Nov-ember'. Reading never gave me any trouble. But whether they could read the words or not, it was unlikely that anyone would forget to celebrate Guy Fawkes Day. For more than a week we had all been busy making our guys from pairs of old trousers and jerseys stuffed with straw and tied together with string. Father would make the head with a ball of rags and a piece of white cloth and paint on it a face complete with eyes, nose, and mouth. When the guy was ready, which was sometimes as much as a week before it was due to be burned, it would be taken from street to street in a small hand cart or propped against a wall with a pipe in its mouth and passers-by would be implored to 'Spare a penny for the old guy'. With the money we collected we bought fireworks.

On November the fifth, as soon as it was dark, Joan and I, Mother and Father, and sometimes Nana and Auntie Noni too, would file downstairs into our tiny backyard where the guy had already been propped up in the middle of the cement floor. After Father had sprinkled him with petrol he was set on fire, whereupon the flames would leap up, the smoke swirl, and the darkness be lit up with a glare of ruddy light in which our faces would glow red and even our voices sound different. Sparklers, which we could run about with in our hands, and Roman Candles and Golden Rain, which had to be set at a distance on the ground, would then be ignited. Catherine Wheels would go whizzing round, broadcasting a shower of rainbow sparks, and rockets go whizzing up into the night. Squibs and crackers exploded at our feet.

In less than half an hour our Guy Fawkes would be blazing merrily; ten more minutes and its head, with charred features no longer recognizable, would fall into the flames, sending up a shower of orange gold sparks. Within the hour the bonfire would have burned itself out and the last flame subsided, leaving only a mass of glowing embers; and standing silent there in the darkness, our shouts and laughter hushed, we would look up through the misty air and see that the stars had come out in the chill November sky.

To what extent London children keep up these old customs I do not know, but I am sure that all their radios, cinemas, and television sets do not give them half the pleasure that we derived from the playing of traditional games and making grottoes and celebrating Derby Day and Guy Fawkes Night.

At this period I never went to the cinema but once. The

film was one of the old, silent Wild Westerns, and I remember how, whenever the hero used his six-shooters, an invisible attendant would fire a blank cartridge. The expected report was usually heard half a minute after we had seen the guns silently spitting fire on the screen.

Our only radio was a long black box with numerous knobs and dials. Once or twice, when my father allowed me to put on the headphones, I heard the voice of Uncle Bob, the first of a long line of *Children's Hour* uncles.

Do London children now ever hear the bell of the muffin-man in distant streets, or see the roast-potato man wheeling his portable brazier round the corner on a cold day? Perhaps they still see the knife-grinder trundling his grinding wheel or the rag and bone man pushing his long coster's barrow on which are the tortoises and goldfish he is willing to give in exchange for scrap iron, old clothes, old newspapers, broken china, and any other household refuse.

But I am sure they never see the lamplighter on his rounds. Even before we left the house at Tooting the old gas streetlights, which on rainy days were reflected in a strange iridescence from the wet pavements, had been replaced by electric standards. As late as eight o'clock in the height of the summer and as early as four o'clock in the depths of the winter, the old lamplighter would come down the street. Having set his ladder against the arm of the lamp-post he would climb up, open the window of the glass shade, light the mantle, adjust the flame and climb down, shoulder his ladder, and be off down the street to the next lamp-post. I am sure that there is nothing lonelier in the world than a deserted street in a big city, dimly lit at intervals by gas lamps.

Not that Joan and I were ever allowed out alone after dark. But sometimes in the summer when it was fully light at six o'clock my mother would send us to the Broadway to meet my father. Tooting Broadway, with its huge statue of King Edward VII in royal robes dominating the latrines and coffee stalls from its marble pedestal in the centre of the traffic island, round which trams would lumber with a dreadful grinding of wheels and screeching of brakes, was to us the hub of the universe. It is, indeed, one of the biggest junctions and busiest shopping centres in the whole of London, though my father could remember how, at the beginning of the century, the High Street had been a country road with green fields on either side.

By the time we were the age he was then the nearest field had retreated several miles, though of course there were Tooting Bec Common and Clapham Common, those green islands in a sea of brick and mortar, where we were taken sometimes in parties to play. There was also Figge's Marsh, where under a charter granted by Queen Elizabeth, an annual fair with swings, roundabouts, and coconut shies had been held for more than three hundred years. Farther afield was Mitcham Common, at the verge of which the Blue House stood in isolation against the sky as though at the end of the world, and Wimbledon Common, where my father had shown me Caesar's Well, with its old Latin letters and figures cut deep into the stones, and where we had tea and plumcake at the Windmill before going down to Queensmere to feed the swans.

As we stood in the vestibule of the tube, waiting for Father to come through the barrier, Joan and I used to feast our eyes on the baskets of apples, oranges, plums, pears, peaches, and strawberries, and on the bunches of grapes and bananas displayed in the window of Walton the Fruiterers. Every time a strong gust of hot air blew across the vestibule from the escalator shaft, which meant that a train had come in, we peered eagerly over the barrier, searching for my father among the crowd that had started pouring through the gate. Sooner or later we would see him, bareheaded and attaché case in hand, coming towards us with his rolling, rather nautical stride, whereupon we would dash forward, seize hold of a hand apiece and lead him home in triumph.

Once in the kitchen, I would open his case and take out the newspaper, which was always *The Daily Herald*, for unlike the rest of the family he was a staunch supporter of the Labour Party, for which he invariably voted. His only concession to Conservatism was to take the *Sunday Express*, a paper Nana also read. Later on, I do not know why, he changed to the *People*. My own interest in the *Daily Herald*, which I read spread out on the floor, it being far too big for me to hold at arm's length, was strictly nonpolitical. I was interested in following the adventures of Bobby Bear. Only after informing myself of the latest activities of this hero did I turn to the news. It was Father's newspaper, I think, rather than from any school primer, that I learned to read.

The first real book I ever handled must have been the old family Bible, so big and heavy I could hardly lift it, with tooled leather cover and gilt clasp which, imitating my father, I called grandmother's Bible, the old volume having belonged to his maternal grandmother. The illustrations with their rich blues, reds, and yellows, depicting Daniel in the lions' den kneeling among skulls and ribs, and Samson with the jawbone of an ass in his hand, had long been familiar to me. One rainy day when I was five or six years old, it occurred to me that instead of merely looking at the pictures I could read the text, and I promptly spelled my way through the first and second chapters of Genesis.

If the Bible gave me my first experience of prose, it was from a prayer-book that I had my first taste of poetry. Inside a cupboard in the sitting-room among my father's books, I discovered at the age of six or seven a volume entitled *Prayer and Praise at Eventide*. From the inscription on the fly leaf I gathered that it had been presented to my paternal grandfather by his mother. Opening it, I came upon the lines:

> *Stay, pilgrim, stay!*
> *Night treads upon the heels of the day.*

This was the first time I had ever met a metaphor and I can still recall the shock of delight the experience gave me. Though I read the rest of the volume, even the prayers, none of it had for me the magic of those first two lines.

Nana visited us once a week on the day she came from Southfields to Tooting to see her old friends, collect her rents, and do a little shopping. Auntie Noni came less often. With the exception of Father's friends and their wives, nearly all the other visitors were Mother's relations. The most frequent and regular of these were Auntie Kate and Auntie Jessie, who came once every three weeks, usually on a Friday and invariably together.

Only the creator of the aunts in *The Mill on the Floss* could have done them justice, though they had neither of them the formidability of Aunt Glegg nor the airs and graces of Aunt Dean. Except that Aunt Jessie was taller, in form and features they resembled each other. In fact the family likeness between all the brothers and sisters was amazing.

Auntie Kate, who could not quite be called stout, had a watery blue eye with a twinkle in it and wore her hair in a bun kept in position by large hairpins which I always tried surreptitiously to pull out. Her nose, which being the family nose could only be called long, was red at the end and shiny, for despite the expostulations of Auntie Jessie and Mother she refused to powder. Their epithet for her was 'old-fashioned', which hardly was matter for astonishment since she was the eldest of the sisters and had already married and given birth to a son when my mother, who was the youngest, was still in the cradle.

Auntie Kate was in fact an old-timer in many ways. She liked a thing no worse for having a patina on it, and invariably preferred the old to the new. Even the sweets she brought us were of a kind which must have been on the market in Dickensian times. Her ginger biscuits were the hardest and hottest I have ever tasted and usually had to be broken with a hammer. Her sense of humour, too, was rather ripe, not to say ribald, and while on holiday at Brighton she used to send all her friends and relations rather broad picture postcards depicting enormously fat women in bathing costumes with exaggeratedly prominent posteriors; so broad, indeed, both pictures and letterpress sometimes were, that old Mrs Bareham at Shoreham, with whom both my parents and Auntie Kate stayed at different times, once told my father: 'My dear, I'm afraid to pick them up off the mat in case I burn my fingers!' Yet Auntie Kate was a victim of melancholia, and in later years used to spend her evenings reading murder stories after which she would put out the light and sit in the darkness for hours on end. She also talked of committing suicide. But at the period of which I am speaking she was a cheery soul and I looked forward immensely to her visits. For many years she was the only aunt whom I suffered to kiss me or whom I consented to kiss for, despite my intense dislike of this form of salutation, I could never resist the breezy way in which she offered her cheek with a 'Come on, lad, give us a banger!'

Auntie Jessie's epithet was 'stately', even as Auntie Lil's was 'refined' and Mother's 'vivacious'. She had a full bosom, kind brown eyes, a musical voice, and was always redolent of scent and powder. Moreover she was quiet and gentle, with a touch of sadness in her expression. Unlike Auntie Kate she relished a ribald joke well enough to laugh at one but not well enough to tell one, and while laughing she always put her hand up to her mouth as if to hide either a blush or her rather prominent false teeth. It was she, not my mother, who amidst the giggles and titters of the sisters would slap at Auntie Kate with her glove and cry: 'Oh, don't, Kate!' when the latter's broad stories went too far.

On their visiting days they usually arrived early in the afternoon; but sometimes they came at eleven o'clock, on which occasions Auntie Kate would scandalize my mother and Auntie Jessie by producing her own lunch, which usually consisted of bread, cold meat or cheese, and pickles from a paper bag. Perhaps my mother's cooking was not old-fashioned enough! Both of them were always very well dressed. After taking off their gloves but not their hats, they would settle down with my mother to discuss clothes and husbands, during which proceedings numerous cups of tea would be drunk. It was one of the mysteries of my boyhood how they could talk for so many hours without stopping. From what I overheard of their conversations I gathered their husbands were rather deplorable creatures, though Auntie Kate and Auntie Jessie were both unanimous that my mother had been much more fortunate in that respect then themselves.

Auntie Kate's husband, Uncle Dan, was an Irish Catholic. He was six foot tall with steel-grey eyes, craggy jaw, and ruddy face, and he smelt very strongly of pipe tobacco. His temper was extremely violent, and he had treated Mother, when she had lived with him, and Auntie Kate before her marriage, with great brutality. A well-known Trade Unionist, he played a prominent part in the General Strike. My father, rather diffidently, once asked him whether Lord Beaverbrook's accusation that the Communists had promised him £25,000 to engineer the strike, was true, but he only laughed, puffed at his pipe and replied: 'If they did I haven't seen any of the money yet'. When I was much older, he offered to get me into the co-operative movement, and thence push me through the trade unions into politics.

Uncle Charlie, Auntie Jessie's husband, was a sporting type, with light brown hair, features inflamed with drink, and a thick utterance. He was related to the proprietor of a chain of butchers' shops in one of which he worked as manager. Unfortunately he could not resist the temptation of levying an unauthorized tax on the daily takings, in which connection he had several times been in serious trouble.

When they had at last finished discussing the merits and demerits of their husbands the three sisters would try on one another's hats, for they all frequently bought new ones, and at each meeting at least one hat was produced which at least one sister had not seen. This ritual accomplished, Auntie Kate and Auntie Jessie would pull on their gloves, pick up their handbags, and, after kisses all round, depart to catch the tram which would take them home.

At that period Auntie Kate lived, as she had always done, at Fulham and Auntie Jessie a little further afield at Hammersmith. Perhaps twice or thrice a year Mother took me by tram to Fulham, which then seemed a very long journey, and on one occasion she left me to stay with Auntie Kate for a whole week. Of this visit, which belongs to my fourth or fifth year, I remember only the pranks I played. Besides pulling out Auntie Kate's hairpins, I tied her to the armchair in which she had her afternoon nap, locked her in the kitchen, opened the door of the chicken coop so that her white hen escaped over the wall into a neighbour's garden, and no doubt committed a score of other villainies. But whatever I did Auntie Kate never minded. In fact she always laughed, for out of the abundance of her good nature she was indulgent to the point of actually enjoying my naughtiness.

But though this is the oldest of my Fulham memories it

is not the clearest. Much vivider is our alighting from the tram and hurrying over Wandsworth Bridge. Somehow it always seemed to be raining, or if it was not raining the sky would be gloomy and overcast and there would be the suspicion of a drizzle in the air. In fact I do not remember that we ever had fine weather when we went to see Auntie Kate. Even if we got on the tram in sunshine, we would be sure to have to get down from it in fog. A blue sky at Tooting Broadway meant black clouds over Wandsworth Bridge.

As we crossed the river we entered what was almost another world. It was not the barges moored at the water's edge, nor the tall white cranes that loaded and unloaded them from the shore, neither the grey gulls wheeling above our heads, but something deeper than all these yet inclusive of them, which made me feel that the atmosphere of Fulham was as different from that of Tooting as that of London was from Pekin's. In what that atmosphere consisted, or how it should be best described, even now I cannot tell. But as I write these lines the dreary, sooty, mournful, decayed, and desolate atmosphere of the Fulham streets comes palpable upon me, and once again I hear the sound of a tugboat siren in the distance like the wail of a lost soul.

Once over the bridge we were not far from Auntie Kate's house. As we passed, block by block, those rows of sordidly respectable houses where, at six o'clock on a cold December night, one might well be tempted to murmur

The winter evening settles down
With smell of steaks in passageways,

Mother would point out to me one house, bigger than the rest, which occupied a unique place in her affections. This was the house where she was born, and in which she had lived with her brothers and sisters until, on the death of their father, the family had been broken up.

The sight of the old house sometimes revived memories, and Mother would begin to talk about her grandfather who had been born in Hungary and who could speak only a little broken English and in whose sweet-shop she had sometimes helped as a girl. Father, to whom she always related these memories, used to tease her by saying that she had surely eaten more sweets than she had ever sold, an accusation which Joan and I always laughingly supported. But Mother's tenderest memories were of her father who, she wistfully recalled, had called her his little fairy. This reminiscence, too, made us shout with laughter and we professed to be unable to understand how anyone could ever think of describing Mother as a fairy. But without heeding us she would go on to relate, with a kind of dreamy pleasure, how when he was resting on the sofa after lunch she would receive permission to slip her hand into his pocket for a penny. However often she asked, she averred, she was never refused. At this point we would declare our conviction that Mother used to take advantage of his drowsiness to extract not the penny to which she was entitled but a sixpence. 'Oh no,' she would say, 'Never!' Why we laughed at her so much when she indulged in these pathetic memories I do not understand. Perhaps unconsciously we wanted to disguise the fact that Mother's feeling for her father had really moved us very much. Like many English folk, we tended to shrink from all exhibition of emotion, especially of the tenderer sort, and to camouflage our susceptibility to it with an affectation of callousness. This grandfather, whom I never saw, for he died when Mother was fourteen, was a celebrated clarinettist and one of her earliest recollections was of being seasick during the Channel crossing when she accompanied him to a continental recital.

Most of her other memories related to her brothers and sisters of whom, including herself, there were fourteen.

Uncle Bert, the eldest, was employed as a departmental manager in a famous London store. Between him and Auntie Kate, the next sister, there was no intercourse as she refused to speak to him because of his culpably unfilial behaviour at the time of their father's death.

Uncle Dick, who with the exception of my mother was the youngest, was a clarinettist like his father. At the age of sixteen he went to India, where he joined the staff of the Governor of Bengal and married. He was the innocent cause of the cruellest disappointment of my boyhood. When I was six he returned to England on leave. The news of his arrival threw me into a fever of excitement, for I assumed he would be accompanied by a whole retinue of Indian servants and, never having set eyes on an Indian before, I therefore looked forward to his coming to the house with the keenest anticipation. But as the sitting-room door opened and I craned my head forward for a glimpse of the

Dusky faces in white silken turbans wreathed

which I hoped to see beaming over his shoulder, all I saw was the very European features of Uncle Dick, Auntie Dolly, and my two cousins. When, a year later, Uncle Dick returned to Calcutta, he left behind a trail of unpaid bills which, to salve the family credit, Auntie Kate and Uncle Jack paid, and it was a long time before any of his brothers or sisters heard of him again.

Uncle Jack, who was the second youngest surviving brother, was accountant in a City firm. He had at one time suffered from a kind of religious mania, which took the form of falling on his knees in the street and praying aloud and of calling out to the passers-by that the Second Coming was at hand. By the time I began to be acquainted with him he had recovered from this harmless affliction, but still taught in Sunday School, and it was he who presented Joan and me with our first Bibles, a green one for me and a plum-coloured one for her. He was a good, kind, gentle soul, though quite ineffectual, and as the years went by he became more and more prone to fits of absent-ness from which he could only with difficulty be recalled.

His wife, Auntie Hilda, was plump and very pretty, and of a disposition almost angelic. Their only child had died very young and the bereaved pair used often to calculate when Joan's age or mine was mentioned, how old 'ours' would have been if he had lived.

Of Uncle Tom and Uncle Harry, neither of whom I ever saw, I know only that the former was killed in the Great War and that the latter emigrated to Australia and became a sheep-farmer. About the twins who died young, and about my grandmother who died not long after my mother's birth, I know nothing at all.

By the time we reached Auntie Kate's door I would have absorbed a good deal of Mother's family history.

The interior of the upstairs flat which she occupied (her son and his red-headed wife lived downstairs) was, like Auntie Kate herself, old-fashioned. The curtains were old-fashioned, the tablecloth was old-fashioned, and even the dog and the cat, an enormous tabby, were old-fashioned. Several years later she and Auntie Jessie went to live in the upper and lower flats respectively of a house down a quiet turning nearby, not far from their old home. But despite the comparative modernity of this house, to such an extent was Auntie Kate successful in impressing her old-fashionedness on her surroundings that to go upstairs to her flat after visiting Auntie Jessie, who had an electric cooker, was like stepping into H.G. Wells's Time Machine and going back into the Victorian past.

At Christmas time representatives of both Father's and Mother's families would be invited to the house, but Mother often used to complain that 'her side' was being neglected. Father's family, which for practical purposes consisted of Nana and Auntie Noni, being not only more compact but geographically more accessible, was, in fact, more frequently invited, for whereas Mother's sisters and their husbands came to tea or dinner in rotation, Nana and Auntie Noni came every time. Of course there was never any serious disagreement between my parents on this point, but I was always conscious of the fact that in my mother's mind at least a certain amount of tension existed between the claims of the two 'sides'.

Preparations for Christmas usually began with the purchase of large quantities of holly and mistletoe from a barrow in the vicinity of Tooting Broadway, where the brightly lit shop windows already glittered with tinsel and where, during Christmas week, the slow-moving crowds of cheerful shoppers thronged the pavements more and more densely every night. The peak period was, of course, the last Saturday before Christmas, when, with the help of Nana's expert eye, we bought the turkey, and when the last stir was given to the Christmas pudding, on which Joan and I had already been working for weeks as hard as we could.

In the kitchen and sitting-room Father would put up paper chains, which we sometimes made ourselves from slips of coloured paper, Chinese lanterns, bunches of balloons, and paper bells. There was always a Christmas tree, which we decorated with iridescent globes of coloured glass saved from year to year, candles of red, blue, green, and yellow wax, and strings of tinsel. The lower branches hung with presents, while at the top of the tree glittered a large tinsel star. One afternoon shortly before Christmas, Joan and I would be taken to one or other of the large department stores, such as the Co-op at Upper Tooting and Holdron's at Balham, where, at the end of our ride through Fairyland, Father Christmas would give each of us a parcel, a pink one for Joan and a blue one for me.

When we were very young we firmly believed in the existence of this mythical personage, every year making out for his benefit a list of the presents we wanted. This list, accompanied by a letter, we posted up the chimney, down which, we were assured, he would come sliding on Christmas Eve to fill the stocking we had hung up before going to sleep. At what age I found out that Holdron's Father Christmas was only one of the shop assistants dressed up, I do not remember, but certainly neither of us was any the better for the discovery.

Whatever the source of our present, which after our disillusionment were inscribed with the name of the giver, the first thing we did when we awoke in the morning was empty our stockings, in the toe of which there was always a tangerine, and open the parcels heaped on a chair at our bedside. I do not remember that anyone in the house went to church on Christmas Day, though Nana probably did, but when I was fourteen or fifteen Mother and Father went to the midnight service. The morning was spent in the sitting-room, where there were dishes of nuts and fruit and packets of figs and dates and where, at midday, Joan and I would be given a glass of wine to drink with our mince pie.

Due to the length of time required for cooking the turkey, which had to be roasted for several hours, Christmas dinner was a late meal, being served usually not before two o'clock. Flushed and triumphant, Mother would emerge amidst clouds of steam from the kitchen, where there had been anxious consultations with Nana as to the precise moment at which the succulent fowl should be taken from the oven, bearing the turkey, a spring of holly stuck in its breast, before her on a large oval dish.

After dinner, which lasted for upwards of two hours, we adjourned to the sitting-room, where the presents were untied from the tree and distributed. Sometimes Father played his favourite gramophone records, among which I remember an operatic aria sung by Caruso of whom he was very fond, and Gershwin's *Rhapsody in Blue* which, from the way in which the clarinet climbed up the scale in the opening bars, I called 'the aeroplane'.

Boxing Day was always spent at Southfields, where we ate what was really a second Christmas dinner, complete with pudding. In her younger days, when Father was still a lad, Nana had cooked five or six Christmas puddings every Christmas, keeping the extra ones for birthdays; but now she did not feel equal to making more than one a year. Her speciality, though, was cakes, jellies, and trifles, of each of which there would be nearly a dozen varieties at tea-time, besides savouries.

The best Christmases, of course, were those on which there was a fall of snow and when, on Father's opening the front door for us to go out and make snowballs, our eyes would be struck by the dazzle of whiteness that made us blink. But whether we were at home or at Nana's the evening would be spent round the fire where glasses of wine stood warming on the hearth and where chestnuts fizzled and popped in a shovel between the bars of the grate.

A few days later came New Year's Day, which as a boy Father had celebrated by ringing the Tibetan ritual hand-bell and exploding crackers outside the front door, a tradition which he would have kept up if Nana and her Southfields neighbours, who were more elderly and more definitely middle class than those of Tooting, had been prepared to tolerate the racket.

Birthdays were celebrated in the same way, though on a much less lavish scale, turkey and Christmas pudding being replaced by the cake with an appropriate number of candles and our name embossed in coloured icing, and instead of the assembly of grown-ups there would be a